CREATED by GOD

CREATED by GOD
Pastoral Care for All God's People

PEGGY WAY

CHALICE
PRESS
ST. LOUIS, MISSOURI

Biblical quotations, unless otherwise noted, are from the *New Revised Standard Version Bible*, copyright 1989, Division of Christian Education of the National Council of the Churches of Christ in the United States of America. Used by permission. All rights reserved.

"Lullaby (40 lines)," on the dedication page, copyright 1940 & 1968 by W. H. Auden; "Musee des Beaux Arts," on page 47, copyright 1940 and renewed 1968 by W. H. Auden, both from COLLECTED POEMS by W. H. Auden. Used by permission of Random House, Inc. All rights reserved.

"Cardinal," on page 129, copyright 1995 by Howard Moss. Used by permission of Richard Evans, executor of Howard Moss's estate. All rights reserved.

"Up Against It," on page 12, copyright 2002 by Eamon Grennan. Reprinted from *Still Life with Waterfall* with the permission of Graywolf Press, Saint Paul, Minnesota.

Excerpts from "At the Fishhouses" on pages 163 and 165 are from THE COMPLETE POEMS: 1927-1979 by Elizabeth Bishop. Copyright ©1979, 1983 by Alice Helen Methfessel. Reprinted by permission of Farrar, Straus and Giroux, LLC.

Cover art: Detail from stained-glass window, Trinity Lutheran Church, Valley City, ND; Photo © Crosiers
Cover and interior design: Elizabeth Wright

Visit Chalice Press on the World Wide Web at
www.chalicepress.com

10 9 8 7 6 5 4 3 2 1   05   06   07   08 09

Library of Congress Cataloging–in–Publication Data

Way, Peggy.
    Created by God : pastoral care for all God's creatures / Peggy Way.
        p. cm.
    Includes bibliographical references.
    ISBN 13: 978-0-827204-97-3 (pbk. : alk. paper)
    ISBN 10: 0-827204-97-3
    1. Pastoral care. I. Title.
    BV4011.3.W39 2005
    253—dc22

                                                    2004025379

Printed in the United States of America

But in my arms till break of day
Let the living creature lie,
Mortal, guilty, but to me
The entirely beautiful

—Auden (1991, 871)

Inviting
theological conversations about care

These essays in a practical theology of care are offered
with remembrance and gratitude for

Seward Hiltner,
whose shepherding perspective was intended
to reflect on and create theology;

Bernard Meland,
whose empirical realism has been neglected
as a foundation for the practice of ministry;

Bill, Rebecca, and Steven Way,
whose love and care were and are unconditional,

and dedicated to

the many laypersons in my adult education classes
who intend to live caring and faithful lives
and understand them theologically;

especially to the faithful laypersons of my Nashville church,
whose struggles to be "A Caring Community of Equality and
Grace" embody many of the perspectives of these essays.

CONTENTS

Invitation to Conversations about Care

While I was writing these essays I worshiped regularly with a congregation in Tennessee. The congregation's mission statement was posted on the outside welcoming board: *A Caring Community of Equality and Grace.* As they lived and struggled to embody this vision, I saw being enacted many of the perspectives of these essays.

Early in my sojourn there, I was moved when a middle-aged woman and her sister with Down's syndrome read the scripture together, a harmony of clear and halting voices. When I was asked to preach, one of the men built a ramp so I could preach from the pulpit; I did not have to request this. Every Sunday and every Wednesday evening there was time for prayer. Participants lifted up the names of the dead and the dying, their survivors, the persons experiencing crises and the aftereffects, and particular situations of suffering throughout the city and broader world. At each gathering was a pause to remember brothers and sisters experiencing the woes of finitude, the agonies of limitation, the "caughtness" of living with chronic illness or in situations that never seemed to get better, and the intrusion of crises: unexpected, unplanned for, unwanted. Victims of violence were routinely mentioned, as were feelings of fear in an unsafe world and concerns for peace in the midst of wars.

Each of these essays seeks to connect a practical theology of pastoral care with the ordinary world of congregations where the woes of a people are recognized; where search for succor and healing goes on, whether human or Divine; and where the quite extraordinary issues affecting culture, theology, and the nature of God are present in everyday discourse.

I was also present when the congregation somewhat unexpectedly had to deal with a particular issue of inclusion. After selecting the top candidates from a field of over fifty to be interviewed for a new position as associate pastor with particular duties in the area of children's and family ministry, the top candidate shared that she was lesbian. Unlike many churches, this congregation had not done extensive Bible study in the area, but was well aware that one of the denominations with which it was affiliated forbade any such hiring practice. This situation raised the need to connect their *vision* ("A Caring Community of Equality and Grace") with their *practices* ("What does that really mean?…Does that really mean *this*?")

These essays do not have a particular interest in issues relating to human sexuality. The concern is rather a deeper issue of how congregations are to connect their liturgies with their practices, their mission statements with their actions, their scriptural knowledge with their ordinary and everyday behaviors, and their intentions with their embodiments. For these issues are directly connected to understandings of care and pastoral care, especially as they focus around identity and community life, ethical discernment and public dialogue. Yet these situations of finitude and limitation, community conflicts and public discord, occur in a context that not only professes, but also expects, to experience the joys of discipleship and the goodness of God. In fact, the essays will argue toward a definition of pastoral care as bearing faithful witness to the joy of creation and the goodness of God.

The congregational leadership recognized that the reflective and decision-making processes would take time. Within those processes, without necessarily being named, were understandings of identity, sexual identity, and the expectation that Christian identity should receive strangers. There were implicit expectations of community: how we were to live together with radically different and frequently incompatible points of view. They participated in ethical discernment and struggling to understand right actions and what is true; as well as the ethics of asking a person who is lesbian to offer leadership in family ministries. They pondered their role in relation to the broader community and the implications of taking a positive action to hire her on the vocations of some of the members who had denominational employment and public political involvements.

Following potlucks and at specially called meetings, in Sunday school classes and worship experiences, the congregation struggled to do right but not to be God. The issue became pervasive in the life of the church; action had to be taken; it could not be referred to a study committee. Was the issue one of doctrine or of friendly disagreement? What costs were involved and what, after all, *were* the costs of discipleship? What were the issues of justice and care? Did care in one arena mean lack of care in another? Would an act of justice (in hiring her) be an act of injustice toward those who would then feel they had to leave their beloved church?

Persons cared deeply and differently about these issues. They struggled with how far boundaries stretch in deciding issues of inclusion, and, without naming it, were working on deep issues of how exclusion and embrace are to be interconnected. One leader in the congregation reminded the body that it had been the first in its region of its denomination to welcome "negroes" into membership, and to those who were afraid that they might become a gay church, he noted that they had not become an African American congregation; in fact, they were still hoping that more persons of other races would come! Like a seminary class without a professor, they struggled with the meaning of words like *equality* and *grace* and pondered what scripture *really* says. The expression "What Would Jesus Do?" (WWJD) was heard.

Personal stories were shared, and several members spoke openly about their own sexual orientation. The young people expressed their disgust that this was an issue at all—just go ahead and hire her! Those in charge of liturgy and music shaped worship services that reflected the congregation's need for care and guidance, trust and forgiveness, courage and patience, struggle and faithfulness in the midst of pondering how to live out their own statement of mission. During this rich and difficult period, members and friends of the congregation continued to become ill and die, experience various crises, live on with chronic inabilities to hear or see or walk, and a war-torn world continued to be lifted up in prayers for peace and justice. The pastors and several others participated in a demonstration against capital punishment in connection with the pending execution of a man in the Tennessee prison system.

These central issues may not surface in the same places as they did at the Tennessee church. After the events of September 11, many congregations had to reconsider their practices of having or not having the country's flag in the sanctuary. A congregation I know of is presently entangled in a controversy over whether human sexuality education can occur on Sunday mornings or only on weekdays. Another fights over whether Christian education should be offered during, or separate from, the community worship experience; and in yet another, a valued member is convicted of embezzlement. These are all issues that demand new thinking about definitions and practices of pastoral care, and new ways to connect the familiar practices of care with the cultural issues that are presently engulfing the broader community and world.

The introduction sets the stage for our reflections. It begins with a description of the partners, cultural contexts, and modes of care. To consider the basic meaning of care is to realize it is not a specialized profession and does not require ordination. Care in the Christian community requires the partnership of all the baptized.

Having raised the question of the basic meaning of care, the first movement of these essays considers those perennial issues of life and death, crisis and chronic illness, disaster and forms of violence, that impact pastoral care and cry out for theological grounding. These are dimensions of the invaluable ordinary work of every congregation. Each essay will reflect on related caring practices, their theological groundings, the challenges presented to contemporary theological understandings, and the role of the many partners in caring processes.

The second movement considers those issues of identity and community, ethics and public discourse, that are intertwined with the first but more related to issues of relationship than to finitude. Issues of ethics and public discourse may not be seen to be related to pastoral care at all! These essays will insist on their intrinsic connection.

The third movement, after encountering the woes and contradictions, searing losses and horrendous evils, disappointments in outcomes and shattered expectations, will define pastoral care as seeking to witness to the joy that the faithful are promised and the goodness of God available for everybody.

Thus the essays intend to simulate conversations that will clarify the theological groundings for congregations not only to *do* care, but to *be* caring places, understanding the costs and the joys of such faithful living. In order to accomplish this, the essays will (1) connect congregational care with the many partners of the caring networks that seek a humane culture; (2) connect congregational care with four of the cutting-edge intellectual/cultural/theological issues that are generally agreed to be central to the cultural dynamics in the twenty-first century: issues of globalization; pluralism and diversity; violence, especially as connected to religion; and changing perspectives in science and technology; (3) connect congregational care with the rich and diverse history of pastoral care practices throughout history and, out of this history, recognize new opportunities for new practices and the formation of caregivers; and (4) invite new ways of thinking about care, as well as recognizing new resources, new perspectives, and new possibilities in responding faithfully, realistically, and creatively to the woes and gifts of the human creature…perhaps even with humility and vulnerability!

The Many Partners of Care

Whether caring in the areas of death or divorce, personal crisis or family breakdown, lack of medical insurance or children's dreams after witnessing an act of violence, there are many caring partners. One way to illustrate this is to consider the many acts of care when an elderly member of a congregation is dying. Thoughts of her or him are lifted up in prayer, with requests for healing and support for the family. Food may be brought to an elderly spouse, support offered in making hospital visits, listening to his or her concerns and grievings. A pastor may take initiative in carrying news. If a hospital is involved there will be experiences of caregivers among the medical personnel, certainly the physician whose medical practices and caring manners are integral to cure and care. Recently we have learned once again that many nurses wish their caring practices to be more clearly offered within an ecclesial context; in some parishes, there may be a parish nurse who has monitored blood pressure, and who may now be alert to the needs of the spouse. Hopefully the variety of technical personnel in the hospital are trained to be hospitable and caring; many understand their jobs as also their vocations, and the tone or manner of their services and presence affects the whole situation.

Perhaps hospice has been or will be involved, with a community seeking a good death and care expressed through relief of pain, the refusal of abandonment, and the acceptance of death processes. In the hospital there may have been an ethical issue raised about the termination of life, and the person will have signed forms having to do with living wills and life support systems. If there is any ethical concern about end of life issues, the chaplain may have been called in for consultation, and may also be a valued presence in the situation of a difficult dying. The chaplain may also be a caring presence among the medical personnel on the floor, for they too may need care.

Or a nursing home may be involved, where attendants making minimum wage may be the primary caregivers, caring for the body as it loses control, becomes dead weight, does not respond. Many of these underpaid attendants are living out a vocation to be caring; persons such as these spend more time in hands-on caring practices than do either other caring professionals or family members.

If the person dies, there may be grief counseling and an awareness of the meaning of loss among family members. A survivor may slip into clinical depression necessitating a medical referral, or experience extreme sadness that a family physician may seek to assuage, even as friends seek to visit, and wait, and hope with the person for the return of better days. Someone beyond the family may help to make decisions with the survivor about housing, or other matters that the death raises. Perhaps the one who dies is the only one who drove the car, or cooked.

Along the way are involvements of various public authorities, such as insurance representatives, who take and keep records on Medicare and private insurances. An entire public sector of Social Security and affordable insurance may have been related to this particular situation; government funding may be helping to support the care received in the hospice or nursing home, and, for some, government benefits may help provide for in-home care, transportation, wheelchairs when needed, and medication.

For this particular situation where prayers have been offered, the caring processes are thick and deep and the partners of care are diverse and crucial for both good dyings and hopeful livings.

When care is understood primarily within psychological and counseling perspectives, much of this thickness and depth is minimized and the role of caregiver made invisible or trivialized. After recognizing the efficacy of the physician and other medical professionals, the layperson who pushes the wheelchair in the nursing home and who patiently keeps the body clean may be as vital a participant in the caring process as the professional or family member. A theological definition of care will define this and be a grounding in each essay that follows.

First, care is a human, and not professional, function. For the human, care is a biological imperative, intrinsic in the creation of the human infant as helpless and as needing physical and emotional caring practices to survive. Because of the nature of our biological/chemical creation, care is a tremendous and terrible burden for the human creature. Regardless of gender, class, ethnicity, race—to be human is to have been cared for, and, the essays will argue, to become human is to be expected, invited, and able to offer care. The need for care is a given and not an option, and there is no privileged place within the human developmental processes where care is not needed.

Second, in Christian theology care goes with baptism and not ordination. A misplaced identification of care with the ordained has made care a matter having a special gift of knowledge. This was perpetuated through definitions of pastoral care as that offered by official representatives of God. When clergy became enamored with the psychological sciences, care tended to be identified with counseling and the need to have specific training in order to be a caregiver. Certainly such perspectives sought to guard against misuse and ignorance, as well as contributing to dynamic understandings. However, psychological knowledge did not guarantee that boundaries were not violated, as indicated by the present scandals in the Roman Catholic Church, where bishops depended on psychiatric understandings to guide their decisions. At present, required boundary training within most Protestant denominations witnesses to the ongoing need to protect the laity from the abusive power of the clergy!

The point here is simply that ordinary care became neglected, if not disdained. Further fractures affected its practices. In connection with the unhelpful hierarchy of clergy and laity, another hierarchy developed within clergy, in which a specialized pastoral counselor was viewed as more informed than the local pastor, and the chaplain frequently disdained local clergy for not being familiar with hospital procedures. Recognition of the partnership of care within the many systems of care within a culture is intended to minimize these misunderstandings. Two particular partners are noted here.

The first is the lay professional. Within congregations, a variety of teachers, nurses, physicians, and lawyers seek to embody their faith in their vocational settings. Moreover, the salespeople and secretaries, mechanics and farmers, beauticians and food service workers collaborate in the creation of a civil and humane culture. The second group, referred to above, may be the most important of all, yet have never been considered as full partners in the systems of care. These nursing home employees, hospital technicians, daycare and preschool employees, houseparents in residential settings, and, yes, ordinary laypersons in their ordinary kindnesses toward their sisters and brothers are the most important of all if a culture of care is to be embodied. These persons usually receive the lowest salaries and recognitions, and one of the mixed blessings of modernity is the way in which care has moved toward specialized functions rather than ordinary kindness and considerations. Yet the latter ground a culture and provide continuity in caring places of formation and wholeness. One example is the intensive care offered by teams of special education teachers to some children of parents who have pursued international adoptions. Another is home health care workers who may be making it possible for congregational members to remain at home.

Third, in Christian theology, caregiver and care receiver are viewed as one; that is, those who offer care are also those who need to receive it, and those who receive care are gifted in offering it. There are no permanent roles of caregiver and care receiver. My former church might have understood its mission statement as also including mutuality—a caring community of mutuality, equality, and grace. A person with Down's syndrome was invited and expected to participate and offer her gifts, offering the good news of the scripture to the assembled folk. This not only diminishes the possibility that some groups of caregivers seem to commit the heresy that they are God; it also enriches the possibility that there are many caregivers available in ordinary congregations and in the midst of a culture overflowing with human needs.

Christian care is intrinsically a part of the culture in which it is practiced. This fourth understanding affirms that the practices themselves are affected by their surrounding environments and Christian care also shares a responsibility for humane and caring institutions within the culture in which God's beloved creatures live. Hopefullylaity who practice within public settings carry their grounding perspectives on compassion and God with them. Similarly, practitioners of care are expected to see the full sweep of dynamics impinging on the woes and sufferings of the creatures with whom they work. This leads directly into public discourse, and commitment to maintaining their own agencies' commitments within the legal and social expectations of the public realm. Frequently the public realm will be more compassionate than the places where Christians intentionally practice, as in issues of accessibility, for churches sought exclusion from the requirements of the Americans with Disabilities Act.

These public concerns may include issues about taxation or a state lottery, health insurance and capital punishment, civil rights for persons of homosexual orientation and concerns about minimum wage. Each of the essays is connected to public discourse as integral to congregational issues of pastoral care. This recognizes that the public sector also carries the themes of the Christian faith as they have become part of the historic streams of experience that have found church and culture mutually shaping one another. There may well be situations where public legislation more adequately expresses these commitments than the practices of congregations; for example, pay and benefits for child care workers, the protection of children from abusers within church programs, and so on.

Since September 11 a group of perennial caregivers in the culture has been brought into further prominence—fire and police personnel, specialists and volunteers who fight fires that threaten communities, workers building sand bag protection against raging rivers, the personnel who clean up after the violence of plane crashes and terrorist attacks on buildings—a variety of disaster workers! The relegation of pastoral care to pastoral counseling and privileged care offered to those with time and money to focus on their inner needs has masked the reality of the full needs for the care of all creatures in a perilous world. The surrounding culture must also encounter and care for the perennial predicament of creatures whose created nature makes them vulnerable to shattered expectations and sorrow, radical suffering and horrendous evil. These practices and understandings of care have not previously been integrally connected to those latter concerns, particularly as raised by the events of September 11, 2001.

The Cultural Contexts of Care

That cultural issues affect the practices of care is not new. Issues of poverty, feminism, and racism have impacted pastoral care for decades. Before that they were affected by, and frequently identified with, the cultural disciplines of the various psychologies and personality theories that sought to define the human being. Practices of care in biblical times were wrought in relation to the cultures in which they were immersed. Cultural periods that are now referred to as Reformation and Enlightenment, Social Gospel and Modernism, all carried cultural dynamics that shaped caring practices. And at the same time, church practices were carried in the streams of historical meaning that affected the values and practices of the culture.

Throughout these essays, I will seek connection with four issues that are generally assumed to be shaping the present world in which creatures are destined to live. Caring practices will be relate to these issues as well as critique them, both positively and negatively. The issues I have selected are those of pluralism, violence and its presence in religions, advances in science and technology, and globalization.

Theologian Miroslav Volf (1996) views the central current theological issues as the relationship between identity and otherness and the need for reconciliation among the world's peoples in order to end—or at least stem—the tide of violence. There is clear connection to pluralism and globalization within the tasks of pastoral care as such care seeks to participate in identity formation and community building to live in such worlds, and views its historic focus on issues of personal suffering as connected to the broader world. Congregations work to embody the gospel by receiving strangers and seeking to become communities of equality and grace. Focus on listening to story has established pastoral care as concerned about particularity and the non-reducibility of one human into another.

At the same time issues of regional globalization affect ordinary care, as river towns lose their vitality and their history, as plants take their jobs to other countries, and as interconnections between and among parts of the world previously known only through the reports of missionaries become real with immigration's redefining of the experiences of community.

While the literature of pastoral care under the impact of the cultural issues of feminism has a modest portion relating to violence affecting women, the theological connections between its under-standings and the presence of violence in the world and within religious faiths have not yet fully impacted pastoral care. And while hospital chaplains have been caught up in ethical discernment for several decades, pastoral care itself has not included ethical discourse as foundational. The cultural issues focusing around increased knowledge in the worlds of science and technology affect pastoral care both in its traditional and contemporary caring practices.

However, the intent of the essays to connect such central cultural themes with pastoral care and practical theology is not only for informed caring practices. The themes (pluralism, globalization, violence, and developments in science and technology) also intend to speak of the formation of caregivers through the culture whose care for the creature must include awareness of the context in which its practices occur…and its new opportunities with them. At the same time, theological reflection upon caring practices can make a contribution to the better understanding of, and response to, the issues themselves. Pastoral care is not application—it is creation and critical thought.

The History and Modes of Care

The essays are written out of the streams of the history of pastoral care, and the many modes of care available serve as a resource within the creature's situation.[1] I will illustrate the workings of the various modes of care by reference to my pilgrimage within the church in Tennessee. The people there live out of their history as a congregation, remembering who they have been and understanding what issues affect their future. Within this context they pray for *healing* and engage in healing processes of supporting one another through difficulties and finding ways to be with the dying and the chronically ill and their families. For them healing involves memory—not being abandoned, even when restoration of life or a more perfect condition is not granted. During times of suffering they participate in *sustaining* modes, helping persons keep on keeping on, while experiencing patience and waiting. They keep going in tough times. Both privately and publicly they seek and offer *guidance*…What is the right thing to do in relation to the hiring of a highly competent and recommended person who is lesbian? How are they to discuss this with young

---

[1]The modes of care are further explored by Seward Hiltner (1958), Clebsch and Jaekle (1983), and in the edited work by Gill-Austern and McLemore (1999).

children, with brothers and sisters in congregations who hold to different positions? What moral guidance is offered in relation to war and sexuality, and out of what perspectives? How have the pastors and others in the congregation guided thinking about capital punishment, and the ethical role of participating in public demonstrations?

The congregation intends to seek *reconciliation* between those who leave the church over the issue and those who remain. Their communion ritual includes the words that one should seek reconciliation with the neighbor before coming to the table; they also hope for reconciliation with their valued past and continuing connections. Somewhat to their surprise they find themselves *advocating* for the employment opportunity of a woman of homosexual orientation, as they have advocated for those sentenced to death.

The congregation had decided to seek an associate pastor out of its desire to offer deeper *nurture* to the children and young people of the congregation, as well as to have a staff person developing family ministries. During one of the many conversations concerning her hiring, several women shared stories of having been *empowered* as girls and women through various youth and women's denominational gatherings. One observes many in the congregation nurturing and empowering the pastor's grandchild, who is a person with Down's syndrome, out of a desire to empower her to wholeness and full participation. There were women in the congregation with an active interest in women's *liberation*, and they have read books together and pondered the relationship of their faith to the ordination of women and homosexuals. In their conversations, they related their own professional careers and vocations to women's issues, while intentionally seeking balance between their vocational and family lives. Some in the congregation, without using the word, spoke of the need to *resist* decisions made by churches and denominations to exclude persons based solely on issues of gender or sexual orientation. Decades ago it had resisted the practice of excluding African Americans from membership.

The historic modes of care, each carrying a great variety of practice within them, are *healing, sustaining,* and *guiding. Reconciling* was a later addition. Only recently has *advocacy* been considered a mode of care, and the discipline has differences about this because advocacy might turn away from the field's historic interest in the individual. Feminist scholars suggested *empowerment, liberation, resistance,* and *nurture* as modes of care to enhance caring practices, recognizing shifts in values and needs of those recognizing their need for and seeking care and not to replace the historic modes. I have added *education* as a mode of care, both because of the close relationship between the theories and practices of Christian education and pastoral care, and because educational practices must prepare caregivers and receivers to see need, view themselves as resource, understand context, and have an intentional grounding and foundation in faithfulness. Most recently, through some new literatures and recognition of the importance of public ritual, which follows disaster and death, I have come to view *ritualizing* as a mode of care. When the rituals associated with the events of September 11 (and its remembrance a year later) were intentionally interfaith, a powerful statement about care and violence, identity and God, the reception of otherness, and the need for reconciliation among peoples was not only loudly, but also deeply, made. The diminishment of ritual celebration in some church communities can be viewed as a failure to care for one dimension of the creature, the creature's hungers for belonging and understanding, meaning and place in a frightening world. The various modes of care will be referenced in various ways throughout the essays.

The essays seek to invite and encourage conversations about care...the conversations need to take place among a wide variety of partners. I have tried to organize them so that each is sufficient unto itself, clarifying theological issues as well as the meaning—theological and cultural—of particular issues of care and the role of laypersons in their various settings.

That they are essays and not case studies or skill presentations is intentional. While they seek dialogue among the many resources of care, they do not seek to make a particular connection between, say, a theological concept and a related psychological or sociological understanding, as much of the academic literature does. They do not focus on a particular problem area, such as that of depression, or a particular recipient group, such as women, homosexuals, Hispanics, and so on. Each one may appear to the reader as a strange combination of story and theology, poetry and cultural interpretation, theological ponderings and references to the ordinary world of congregations.

They do intend to move toward a definition of pastoral care as compassionate acts that bear witness to joy and the goodness of God, but there is a long way to go before we dare make such an affirmation when we find that the creature lives within a history that is mundane, boring, ambiguous, exciting, and evil, and a creation where conflict among values, creatures, ecosystems, religions, and nations is the permanent environment of human action while intellectual, spiritual, and physical fragility confine human freedom.

This is the reason for the choice of the Auden poem, for my concern and commitments are for human creatures who are mortal, guilty, *and* entirely beautiful. They are created and placed by divine love and compassion in a world that maintains its beauty alongside its peril for the creature, including terror and violence. The essays will take a clear position that history is not evil, finitude is not sin, and culture is not created and grounded in violence. But it is premature to make such claims. To dare to define pastoral care as intentional witness to joy and the goodness of God can only have integrity when the sufferings to which pastoral care attends are given full voice in the witnessing.

A Theological Anthropology

The Shocks of Finitude and Limitation

The first movement consists of essays on finitude; chronicity; crises; and encounters with violence, terrorism, and evil as connected to the practices and theologies of care.

Each essay expresses something of what the poet Eamon Grennan (2002) has expressed as "the fact of glass" in his poem "Up Against It." I suggest it as a metaphor for human experiences of limitation. As you read, picture the human creature coming up against death and dying, illnesses that don't heal, various crises, and horrendous acts of evil, and experiencing the suffering related to each.

> It's the way they cannot understand the window
> they buzz and buzz against, the bees that take
> a wrong turn at my door and end up thus
> in a drift at first of almost idle curiosity,
> cruising the room until they find themselves
> smack up against it and they cannot fathom how
> the air has hardened and the world they know
> with their eyes keeps out of reach as, stuck there
> with all they want just in front of them, they must
> fling their bodies against the one unalterable law
> of things—this fact of glass—and can only go on
> making the sound that tethers their electric
> fury to what's impossible, feeling the sting in it.

Moses had to recognize that his life would continue only "this side of the Promised Land," and he lived on with his eyes undimmed and his bodily vitality undiminished. Martin Luther King Jr. also glimpsed his promised land—and was assassinated. But his followers continued to confront the evils of racism as they persisted in history. The bees' place and space were limited; so, too, do human persons run up against their own hard "facts of glass."

They do not see visions fulfilled or expectations met.

Yet we care for one another and undertake risky and costly acts of justice in times such as these. Esther faced kingly oppressive power and anti-Semitism, war, and the loss of her own privileged position. In this movement the essays also reflect on the cultural dynamics with which the contemporary creature must cope, globalization and pluralism, frightening and amazing developments in science and technology, as well as experiences of violence and evil and the recognition of such dynamics within religions themselves. We will connect these central issues with the theories and practices of pastoral care.

Another dimension of the reality of finitude and limitation is expressed in the song "I Can't Make You Love Me If You Don't" (written by Mike Reid and Allen Shamblin, recorded by Bonnie Raitt, among others). The creature must learn to receive and cope with the many "no's" that will be heard, expectations that won't be met, visions that do not come into being. We will be defining the creature and the creature's world as defined by mortality and limits, and the underlying question is how are human creatures to care for one another and understand their place in the perilous world in which they are called to care? The four essays will present a view of ordinary caring situations and practices, interpreting them culturally and theologically, and challenging them to be connected to the rich history and many partners of caring processes.

The *first* essay will define finitude and limitation and explain why we refer to the living human creature as mortal, guilty, and entirely beautiful. We will state why we use the language of creaturehood and creaturely stance as we state two types of limitation, biological and historical, and show how they are disclosed in ordinary situations of pastoral care in the everyday life of congregations. We will reflect on what we learn from them about theological understandings, as well as about the creatures who encounter them and the practices that they call forth. Stark descriptions of the creature's perennially perilous situation underlie the essay, as well as introducing the thesis that pastoral care witnesses to joy and the goodness of God.

Second, we will attend to situations of chronic illness, various disablements, genetic or chromosomal accidents, and what it means to live within our genes, when neither prayer nor medical treatment, hard work nor privileged care make things get better. In fact, in many situations of chronicity the situation worsens, not only the health of the afflicted but deterioration within the context of the suffering. We will consider both ordinary situations such as Alzheimer's, and more dramatic situations such as the paraplegia of Christopher Reeves. Chronic situations will disclose not only the creature's suffering, limitation, and finitude, but also a style of consent and courage that allows for faithful living and that may serve as model for all creatures coming up against their various facts of glass. Chronicity may not be primarily curse.

Third, we will explore the nature of crisis and the impact of losing the structure of one's (or one's culture's) life through sudden change and intrusion. Such a sudden change might come because of a natural disaster such as flood, tornado, or hurricane, or because of the intrusion of history as through the suicide bombers at the World Trade Center. The change might be the crisis of a child's death in a pool, the announcement by one partner in a marriage that he or she is leaving, the unanticipated need to attend to the health of a family member, the loss of a job. The focus will be on ordinary pastoral situations, and what we learn from them about a theology of change, as well as faithful ways of receiving and responding to unexpected challenges and unfair demands.

Fourth, we will attend to dynamics of violence and terrorism, and define and take seriously experiences of evil in the creature's life. Situations of horrendous evil and radical suffering will be noted, as well as the seemingly intrinsic presence of cruelty and brutality within historical process, that is, within the human self, the family, the culture—even the religion that is practiced and the faith affirmations that are celebrated.

Each essay in different ways will invite theological ponderings and particular reflection on caring practices. At the end of this movement—the completion of the four essays—a postscript suggests connections to the development of a pastoral theology or a practical theology of care, and suggests what the essays mean for congregation and chaplain, for specialized pastoral counselor and laity living out their ministries in both congregation and the public arena.

Pastoral Reflections on Finitude and Limitation

BIOLOGICAL AND HISTORICAL

No one has ever asked me to preach, lecture, or teach on finitude. Nor have I been asked to propose the skills necessary for limitation counseling, although for years I was involved in growth counseling and wrote my dissertation on that topic.

Yet much of pastoral care is with persons who find that "the air has hardened," or who come up against "the fact of glass" in situations that they see could be different than they are. Finitude—the condition of being limited—marks the human situation. Mortality, the fact of death, defines the human situation. The human creature perennially encounters peril and precariousness, and theology is grounded in the search to make some sense of that situation—and God's participation in it. Some of the reflections on the events of September 11 reflect dimensions of experiencing the shock of finitude.

In congregations the prayers of the people normatively lift up the cries of human creatures struggling with their own and their beloved's mortality. Limitation experienced through illness, crisis, knowledge of violence, terror, and evil in the world brings forth expressions of woe and perplexity. Time spent by the clergy in hospital visits, funeral planning, funerals, and care for survivors occupies a percentage of pastoral time that probably outweighs that devoted to sermon preparation. Training in pastoral and other forms of counseling, such as grief counseling, is expected, and the programs of the church frequently include grief groups, concerned not only with death itself, but with a variety of other dyings and losses in areas such as marriage, job expectations, or even who we wanted our children to be.

The connections of death with the caring practices of ministry underlie every reported form of death in the daily papers, *Time* magazine, and on TV. Not only the peaceful deaths from the obituary pages, but the deaths of the murdered child, participants in traffic accidents, victims of fires and floods find their ways into the awareness of congregations through participation in funerals and ongoing pastoral care. Those choosing the ordained ministry frequently do not realize that they are choosing a lifetime of preoccupation with death in its many forms. In pluralistic culture different practices concerning death must become a part of the knowledge of the chaplain in a children's hospital, where the chaplain becomes liaison between death and the appropriate practices of the many different faith communities involved.

Culturally, pastors and laypersons are involved economically with an entire funeral home industry, and in some churches the budget is affected by income from their cemeteries. A growing grief industry has teams of counselors—a variety of lay professionals in many fields, who listen after crises of school shootings, airplane crashes, terrorist attacks. There are indeed many partners in death, not only medical professionals but also technicians and service personnel of various sorts, morgue attendants, those in charge of preparing graves, sellers of hearses.

This limitation of death, that is, biological finitude, is a dimension of creation itself. The human creature is created to die. We are made up of the same elements in which we live, as Bernard Meland (1962) says in describing that "man is microcosmic as surely as he is individualistic…The seawater flows in his veins. The chemicals and ores embedded in the earth combine to give form and frame to his visible, bodily structure" (201).

Shaped from the clay of the earth, to be human is to be limited biologically and chemically…but also to have our life processes extended and healed through increasing scientific and technological knowledge. Yet death is a constant companion, not to be outlawed or conquered. The events of September 11 were a massive reminder of death, an intrusion into expectations of safety and control. Death is a natural law within created processes.

But there is yet another kind of limitation, which Meland defines:

> The human response to its situation, therefore, is hedged about by two kinds of limitations. 1) the limitation of finitude or creatureliness which applies to all men, and 2) the limitation of the cultural orbit of meaning, which prepares the human mind and psyche within a given area of human association to receive and to react to occurrences in specific and characteristic ways. (Meland, 1976, 122)

But what does this have to do with pastoral care? Care practices are not only attendant on death; they also interpret it. Centuries of interpretation have claimed that death came into the world through sin, rather than being a natural process. Theology continues to spend inordinate energies defining God in relation to God's relationship with death, as, if not causative agent, at least compliant in allowing such an end to the beloved creature. We will reflect on this throughout the essays. Here we note that this understanding of the creature as limited makes sense in ordinary human experience. As the previously mentioned Bonnie Raitt hit states, "I Can't Make You Love Me If You Don't." Indeed! One can't. And lovers discover that they must deal with the otherness—the fact of glass—the limitations of the beloved, even as parents must learn that they do not control the formation of their progeny and cannot even shape them to their own ends. There is good precedent, even in scripture, where the predominant response of the human creature to Moses and Jesus, the prophets and Paul, is *no!*

In struggling to be a caring community of equality and grace, my church experienced the reality of encountering radically different scriptural and cultural understandings of homosexuality that were not interchangeable. Nor were they subject to modification either by overcoming ignorance or by presenting logical arguments. Specialized pastoral counselors have learned that real change occurs only slowly and over time; and ordinary pastors discover that they are joining an ongoing community with stories and a will of its own. Biological and cultural limitations are two facts of existence; that is, they define the creature's biological and historical situations that underlie all of pastoral care. Yet as both Meland and Volf note in different ways, coming to terms with limitation is also a discovery or rediscovery of gifts, possibilities, and opportunities for continuing endeavors for the creature to be at home even in the givenness of its history, and to find joy and the goodness of God there——even after the events of September 11.

Thus we begin with recognition of the complex dance between the human creature realizing that it is not God, but that it is gloriously endowed with human capacities for freedom and moral discernment— for caring, if you will. Pastoral care needs to be grounded in this simple perception that the human person is creature, that is, mortal; that the creature acts imperfectly in the midst of its complex and perilous context, its very development impairing its freedom, that is, it is guilty. And yet it is entirely beautiful, that is, created in *Imago Dei* as a "Thou" by a loving and good Creator. The creature is then lovingly placed into a perilous and precarious historical existence in which God does not abandon it. A theology that interprets death as coming into the world through sin is frequently accompanied by an understanding that the creature is thrown into a broken world either to instigate eternal punishment for the creature, to be assuaged only with God's own second coming, or to make clear the power relationship between creature and Creator. Conversations concerning these theological themes occur throughout the essays, relating them to pastoral knowledge.

In this complex area of finitude and limitation, the creatures, like the bees, frequently buzz and buzz around, pursuing the impossibility of finding some way through the hardened air, of finding someone to blame for the fact of glass. And the ordinary pastor and lay caregivers experience the creatures' cries in the most ordinary and everyday places, hopefully free to express their rage and lament, and hopefully with pastoral persons who can accompany them behind their thin question of "Why did God do this to me?" into the depths and textures of their complex situations. This pilgrimage is informed by reflecting on a creaturely stance; denials of death, limitation, and finitude; legitimate suspicions of limitation; limitation and the modes of care; and the world of the creature.

A Creaturely Stance

To claim creaturehood is to echo the central theme of theology: that the human being viewed as creature is not God. Volf, who in complex ways seeks for humans to imitate God, states that, "There is a duty prior to the duty of imitating God, and that is the duty *of not wanting to be God*. Of letting God be God and humans be humans. Without such a duty guarding the divinity of God, the duty to imitate God would be empty because our concept of God would be nothing more than the mirror image of ourselves" (1996, 301).

But in maintaining the fundamental difference between God and non-god, the gifts of the creature have often been neglected. Particularly following the Enlightenment and well into the last fifty years of the twentieth century, pastoral care sought freedom on the creature's behalf from prematurely imposed views of its finiteness and limitation. In pastoral counseling the individual creature's self was affirmed and resources sought to actualize it; even to speak of creaturehood would seem to be burdened with limitation and refusal to become the optimistic view of human being that prevailed in liberalism.

A postliberal point of view seeks to place the human being as creature at the same time as celebrating the gift of the creature's resources, creativities, and capacities. Indeed the expectations placed upon the contemporary creature to love diversity and seek justice for all demand a creature with the capacity to so act and, if you will, a moral and decisional creature. The theological points are important: that the creature is not self-made or self-named; and that the creature shares in its created being the chemical elements and biological processes of other creatures and of created nature itself. For Meland, the creature is grounded in an elementalism of recognizing that it is born into a particular historical ongoingness and will, without escape, die. Claiming such a creaturely stance in the face of inevitable death and the invariant presence of other creatures, and finding oneself situated in a particular body, family, culture, and historical period frames the context in which pastoral caring occurs. For many— caregiver and care receiver alike—coming to terms with this context and finding within it grace, joy, and forgiveness is itself a caring goal.

Within this context the creature alternates between openness to new possibilities and futures and closedness to change and the risks of learning how to live with others. Theologically this issue impacts ordinary marriage counseling and responses to disaster.

The practices of pastoral care are wrought out in such contexts, just as my church experienced dynamics of openness and closedness in its decision making about hiring a new associate pastor. Both dynamics are a dimension of the human situation, as ordinary pastors find out routinely. Denominational structures and ecumenical organizations know that desired changes cannot be mandated; they are wrought out. The subject of pastoral care is creature, not autonomous human being.

Denials of Death, Limitation, Finitude

There are at least two forms of denial operating, one expressed in the recent Ted Williams story. The other is a more subtle theme that so identifies death with sin, and history with finitude, that culture itself becomes viewed as created and grounded with violence. This leaves the creature without recourse and the meaningfulness of little kindnesses, for the entire context is one of corruption and evil.

On every sports page in the United States, the death of Ted Williams was commemorated. And on the home page of its Web site, the Alcor Life Extension Foundation, a cryonics lab in Scottsdale, Arizona, described its efforts to overcome, through science and wishful thinking, "the event we now refer to as death" (2003).

When that event came to Ted Williams at the age of 83, a *New York Times* reporter noted that "one suspects death needed no exceptions, as Williams was a man who knew how to play by the rules, and dying is every bit as much a rule in life as the foul lines are in baseball. It seems doubly bizarre, then, that Mr. Williams's body has been shipped to Alcor to hang upside down, frozen, until science comes up with a cure for old age" (Sandomir, 2003).

Shortly following this, television told the story of the possibility of turning the body into industrial diamonds, which the survivors could make into jewelry. Being composed of the elements of the earth, there is apparently enough carbon to make about forty diamonds from one body at the cost of about $4,000.

A deep cultural stream of thought in the United States suggests that Americans tend to view illness and suffering and death as anomalies that can be conquered and controlled. This sophisticated and often helpful denial of death can get in the way of encountering creaturehood as a given, even within religious thought. Perhaps the central thrust of religious sensibility has been to create meaning out of the creature's shock at its own finitude, as well as the passing, the perishing, of the objects, institutions, and persons that have defined its identity and been its love objects. This religious sensibility need not be undermined by moving toward a place where death is viewed as a natural process, a dimension of the created order. A congregation might study Dr. Sherwin Nuland's *How We Die* (1994), tracing the processes of the body's lifelong and inexorable movement toward death. A religious sensibility might also note that both what we used to call "primitive folk" *and* postmodern scientists of the present age seek anti-death strategies, as representatives of the latter present cloning and cybernetic strategies as anti-death resources. So death continues to be a reality that the creature seeks to refuse, to deny, to turn into an event that it can comprehend by locating blame for it and devoting itself to conquering it. This can present pastoral problems!

When the battle against death was joined by modern medicine, the interest in palliative care and a good dying was diminished with searches as to how to prolong life. Unanticipated results were that persons died in hospitals, frequently abandoned by family and physician alike, while both physician and family failed in their battle with death. Hospice centers practice death with dying processes openly; after the resources of technology are exhausted, the dying one is attended with love and relief from pain, in the company of family and friends and skilled persons serving as attendants of death, which is, as much as possible, welcomed in its inevitability.

A conference on good dying offered by the Center for Medical Ethics in Kansas City several years ago attracted more than five hundred people. Rich sharing occurred at the conference, which was composed of all religions and faith groups, as well as of the many partners of caring processes. Even the dying themselves were included, in films in which they shared their stories. The meeting pace was rich with multiculturalism and interracial conversation, since death, and its processes, is indeed a universal process. While there were many different theological orientations present, the view of a loving God who is the giver of life and who chose the perishing qualities of earth and sea for the birthing of God's entirely beautiful creature, also marked the proceedings. This turn is away from centuries of misperception theologically of death as punishment or reward, scourge to be hidden away or embarrassment in a post-Enlightenment world. Issues of ordinary pastoral care were of course connected with this. Until recent years, cremation was viewed negatively, as the whole body needed to be present for a bodily resurrection. Yet bodies were blessed with ashes, and dirt was thrown on enclosed and expensive caskets. The structural limitations of the human mind could find no other way to preserve the need for a whole body at the time of a future resurrection. Theological conversation about the body's composition had not yet become possible; my great aunt's leg was preserved at the funeral home until she died, and it could be reunited with her body in the casket in order that she could appear whole before God.

Concern for salvation has created a variety of other rituals intended to ensure the person's continuity, such as dying fortified with the sacrament, and making sure one is born again before the last breath is taken. Pastoral care concerns continue to accompany issues of the death of a fetus or a stillbirth, where issues of baptism, blessing, and naming enter into contemporary caring practices by pastors and chaplains in hospital settings. Theological issues not considered in seminaries have been worked out in the chaplain's places of ministry. A person's need for care has not always matched the faith's openness in offering it.

There have been persistent and damaging understandings of this fact of glass, this hardened air. Suicides were refused burial, as the creature claimed for oneself the power of death. Issues of life and death always mark caring practices, grounded pastorally on the relation of creature to creator. Nor is it surprising that cultural issues impact the death and dying processes. For centuries members of different races had to have different burial grounds, and churches that presently survive on the proceeds from their graveyards are surviving on what was clearly a racist structure. Perhaps a caring practice might be for such congregations to have a ritual seeking forgiveness for their historic participation in such practices; perhaps the congregation's children could play in the cemetery, exploring what is written on the grave markers, remembering and becoming familiar with the history of death.

The identification of death with sin occasioned other practices that have only recently changed. Only a generation ago there were "freak shows" at circuses, where the unfortunate victims of birth defects were secretly and lasciviously displayed for an entrance fee! Bodily imperfection was for generations identified with sin and viewed as punishment. The horror of receiving a deformed infant led to practices of infanticide in various cultures and to holding such secrets deeply within families. Even within church families separate facilities were built for those whose bodies and minds were reminders of the limitation of the body and its genetic and biological chemical base. There are many examples where the refusal of biological limitation has led to an exclusion that "protected" sanctuaries and gatherings of the faithful from those who would remind them of their own mortality, their own fears of the connection between sin and bodily punishment. Bodily limitation remains an impediment to ordination in some faiths, as the ordained must be considered whole before God.

This refusal was integrally connected with the need to protect God from blame in such situations, so complex theodicies sought to explain such painful situations in terms of God's relationship with God's creatures. From this flows the ever-present question hovering within situations of pastoral care in relation to finitude and limitation: Why did God do this to me? Even when mitigated to, "Why did God allow this to happen?" the question carries central perspectives on the complex and profound interrelationships of understandings of the creature, history, culture, world, and the nature of God that are the core of theology. Each essay guides us toward our own understandings as the issues show up in particular acts of care. Church architecture itself stated a preference for the exclusion of those with disabilities. Central church programs of inclusion, such as confirmation, excluded those with developmental disabilities. For, if death and disablement come into the world through sin, then it is either the creature's fault or God must be rationally protected from "his" complicity. Neither provides a gracious theological basis for pastoral ministries in the areas of finitude and limitation, chronicity, crisis, or the presence of violence and evil.

Yet the Creature Often Denies Finitude for Very Good Reason: Rightly Suspicious of Limitation?

Most theologies and pastoral care texts do not begin with this fact of death. Although it preoccupies pastoral care practices, recent years have seen pastoral care's growing identification with the just refusal of certain types of understandings of finitude, limitation, and of the relation of the creature to the Creator and who defines it.

For example, a dimension of creation is the creature's gift of creativity and imagination. Coming into consciousness carries with it the capacity to envision a better world, a better place, the conquering of death, disability, etc. The creatures become righteously angry when barriers are presented to their imaginings. Premature recognitions of limitation have minimized the human gifts intrinsic in creation. Caring practices are diminished when limits are placed on the use of knowledge of the body coming from the human sciences. Organ transplants, *in vitro* fertilization, dialysis, and psychotropic medications are all gifts of human creativity. Only recently have erectile dysfunctions been publicly recognized and healing sought; religious limitations are still placed on research in the areas of human sexuality as theologies have thought morals separate from biology and chemistry.

Caring practices have also been affected by theological limits placed upon human creativity and powers. Only recently have caring modes of empowerment and liberation invited the full participation of women in church and religious life, and this continues to be a central issue of cultural differences throughout the world as growing ecumenical and interfaith caring practices encounters one another. Similarly, in some circles care has come to be viewed as ordinary and everyday when compared to the possibilities for cure. Budgets provide millions for research on technologies of cure, but only pennies for those who need palliative care, or assistance in the tasks of daily survival. Even more recently have caring practices been viewed as necessarily related to ethnic, racial, or economic groups. Here limitation may not be that of creaturehood, but rather that of being oppressed—or made invisible—by those who seek to keep power for themselves. Pastoral care will of course deal with creaturely finitude, but may also join in advocating full inclusion in church and culture, liberation from imposed negative views of self, empowerment to define one's own caring needs, and active resistance to acts of violence. Discerning such difference is crucial to all pastoral care practitioners, which makes inescapable the connections of care and justice.

The creature and the creature's caregivers, themselves creatures, cannot escape these issues of double limitation, that is, of the finitude of biological death and of historical and cultural situatedness. Creatures do not control the nature or practices of history, God, or other creatures. They are limited also in their capacities to understand the whole. A dimension of their creation is a structure of limitation in the capacity for knowledge. Meland's term "margins of intelligibility" states our limitations of understanding without denying our gifts of seeing and of shaping our worlds. Being able to discern when to accept/receive finitude and when to refuse or deny it is crucial in the connection of pastoral care with the emergent cultural issues. Different faiths and cultures will place the margins differently. Emerging knowledge from the physical and social sciences will continue to push our boundaries of understanding. What is perceived as a loss by one cultural group might be perceived as liberation by another.

These issues are also expressed by novelists and journalists, in movies and in the daily newspaper, all witnessing to the awareness of human creatures struggling with understanding who they are, what their place is in the world, and who their gods are. On July 24, 2002, Margalit Fox (2002) quoted Chaim Potok from an unpublished 1992 interview in which he describes his culture of faithfulness:

> It was essentially a fundamentalist atmosphere, which is by definition both joyous and oppressive simultaneously. Joyous in the sense of knowing you belong to some cohesive community that will care for you and in whose celebrations you can participate fully; and who will help you mourn if you need a support group in time of personal tragedy. And repressive because it sets boundaries and if you step outside the boundaries the whole community lets you know. Within such tensions we define and practice care.

Experienced Limitations Call Forth the Full Range of Pastoral Care Modes

Bernard Meland defines his theology as a "brooding kind of inquiry," pushing into depths, textures, and a variety of forms that do not lend themselves readily to understanding or conceptualization. This is the daily work of pastoral care: participating in healing processes even when they become those of dying; providing sustaining services and presence when rapid change or cure is not going to happen; offering palliative care in hospice settings; guiding through the complex ethical questions that accompany issues of limitation, including suicide, assisted suicide, and termination of life support systems; guiding toward participation in liberation processes that refuse premature or imposed limitation and perhaps empowering persons to risk such activities; reconciling not only in relation to acknowledgment of the fact of death and limitation, but also reconciling those with different understandings of what God intends.

It is not surprising that theological and cultural battles are not only about the nature of God, but also about ways in which that conversation becomes political. Care connects particular situations with public discourse; this is so for advocates of pro-life and pro-choice. Here issues of finitude and limitation are wrought out in public; here care issues again connect with cultural and religious values. Yet care remains mostly within the framework of everyday living, nurturing the creatures from infancy through adulthood, in their family and cultural settings. At some points we may seek to ritualize processes, caring for the human need for meaning and understanding, and offering it aesthetically, with wisdom, comfort, and challenge. As a dimension of care, rituals must be truthful to the human situation, not trivializing it or avoiding its brute realities. Exploration of the modes of care and ritual offerings that accompany stillbirth is also an exercise in how best to accompany the creatures receiving what is perhaps their first experience of the shock of discovery of their finitude and limitation.

Certainly in relation to limitations of biological and cultural finitude care should assertively take on an educational function, for this most ordinary topic is seldom mentioned and the creature is not the only structure that is limited; the institutions that the creature creates to care for itself are also limited. A primary example is in contemporary ecclesiology, where the church growth movement seeks to overcome the limited form of churches that are dying. As with those workers in nursing homes who offer the bulk of hands-on care, small and quite ordinary parishes offer the same kind of ordinary spiritual care among hundreds of thousands of parishioners. As they age, and as their churches lose their vibrancy, their ministries are trivialized and no one wants to serve a church full of old people. This ecclesial refusal of finitude focuses upon growth as the highest ecclesial value. There should be a hospice movement for the good dying of churches, who may have lived beyond a certain type of vibrant faithfulness, but who have served well and also deserve to die with dignity and to be celebrated for their historic ministries.

In his *Christian Century* column, Martin Marty reflects on a bias that "Christian gatherings would best serve God if they shunned cornerstone laying, smorgasbords and youth camps," focusing rather on issues of "poverty, rights, welfare." Defending himself against charges that what he says is a "sure sign of the compromising with reality that comes with aging," he states:

> I'd rather plead that we notice how, after 9/11, we were both instinctively impelled and rhetorically nudged to affirm bonds of family, neighborhood and church, across the lines of age, race, sex, income and taste. That is what religion page headlines suggest that local churches are doing. At their best, they are caring for their immediate community while also motivating people to use their religious and communal commitments to move beyond the church basement, the sanctuary or the church yard, and into the public arena and a global mission.

At their best, ordinary congregations are pondering the complex issues of finitude and limitation, and witnessing to the goodness of God in the midst of stillbirth and hospice, violence and public discord. In their everydayness of presence within issues of finitude and limitation, they recognize the elemental dimension of their entirely beautiful creatures. Meland can help us claim this reality:

> By the elemental dimension of existence I mean simply living with an awareness of the fact of birth and death, confronting man's existence, its range of opportunity for human fulfill-ment, not only within these acknowledged limits defined by birth and death, but with creaturely feelings appropriate to them.

Simply living within these limits on a sophisticated level, shunting off emotion, anxieties, and inquiries evoked by an appropriate element, is the usual commonplace pose of sophisticated modernity...Elementalism...is simply a capacity to acknowledge humbly and humanly this fact of existential limitation, defined and symbolized by the events of birth and death, and to experience creaturely feelings appropriate to such limitation and dependence. (Meland, 1976, 165).

Such creaturely feelings ground most pastoral situations. And they occur in many world (or specific and concrete historical) situations that do not yield readily to ground theory.

That kind of a world does not yield readily to grand theory... These essays will be slowly working out an alternative view as we spend more and more time on the experiences of caring pastors and laypersons. The issue is to receive, recognize, and consent to finitude, carefully discerning when it is limitation and when oppression, and then to recognize the possibilities within that givenness. Within this dynamic, to focus on utopian images, expectations of kingdoms and promised lands, only makes things worse...for this obscures or masks the everyday meanings and graces, blessings and gifts that nurture the creature in a nexus of care and affirmation. Moreover, the creature is made of the elements of the environment itself, a dimension of it, in continuities and perishings. The networks of institutions and cultures are to nurture, sustain, and heal the creature's situation of givenness. History is not itself evil, yet not only do the complications of creation lead to bad choices, but bad choices arise out of the same depths of givenness and creation as those that lead to care. Especially within a faithfulness that continually promises, with evidence, God's perennial presence, God's goodness not only in the gift of creation itself (after all, we're here!), which is to be the more powerful? Certainly a dimension of God's goodness is creatures' presence with one another in acts of care in a perilous world.

In this sense, the emergent issues are indeed connected to care: Soon we will look at violence as a dimension of the human condition and pluralism, built into the beginning of struggle between herder and farmer. Science and technology not only raise unprecedented questions, but offer unprecedented opportunities for healing and sustaining globalization that continues to play out the humans' discovery of the hugeness of the world in which the creature has been lovingly placed, not thrown in punishment or as a test of devotion. Surely if the problematics of the human situation are but a never-ending test of the creature's acknowledgment that the creature is not God, there will be little to discover of awe and majesty, beauty and ordinary graces.

Thus the given is not the bad, the evil, but the *is* that the creature is born into. The metaphors and learnings from other times are perennially helpful but also perennially difficult to untangle as the streams of experience that have been carried, and the orbits of meaning have so shaped the creature that it is difficult, if not impossible, to be or to see as the first-century prophet did. Even to capture the "Truth" in a holy text is misleading, as it carries within it the expectation that the insight can be applied, whereas the creature's experiences are continually being negotiated and wrought out, over time, with an admixture of terror and grace, violence and small kindnesses; and always, life goes on. Hopefully, the pastoral caring response is informed by the joy and blessings of a good God continually at both core and horizon of the creature's situation.

What Is This World in Which the Creature Is Placed?

The shock of experiencing the reality of finitude and limitation underlies most pastoral care. Whether situations of death and dying, living with chronic illness, or experiencing the intrusion of crisis or violence—or having to learn to live with other creatures radically different from themselves—the human creature has to come to terms with the limits within itself and its surrounding worlds. The creature has to live within its genes and its histories, the givenness of its situatedness of bodily structure, race and gender, Dow Jones figures, and political party in power.

A host of issues are raised. Where was God on September 11? Or, for that matter, where was God on September 12 when a family somewhere experienced a stillbirth, or later in the month when teenagers were killed in a car crash, or at this moment right now when somewhere persons are dealing with diagnoses of illnesses that will lead progressively, however slowly, toward their deaths?

After September 11, 2002, the first anniversary of that infamous September 11, the headlines of *The New York Times* reported that the country was lamenting two losses: the loss of those who died and the loss of a nation's sense of being a safe fortress. The theological questions that accompany the headline are, "Where was God?" and "What kind of a world is home for the creature?"

Sometimes theologians want to wrap everything up in neat packages…When interviewed, the wife of a hero of September 11 said that she understood that there was a good creation, but because God gave free will, human beings make very bad decisions. If we did not, the world would be perfect. In any event, all would be revealed in eternity, and, for the present, she would go on living her daily life (Herbert, 2002).

This is not far from classical theology. Creation is pronounced "good." To fulfill it, the creature is created from the clay of the earth, and placed in a perfect spot. But, refusing to obey God, the creature loses this idyllic vista and has to live in the world of work and childbirth, of sibling rivalry and conflict between farmer and herdsman, of human violence and natural disaster.

Or, finding oneself lost in chaos and drowning in perplexity, the creature becomes anxious for its own place and, seeking to secure itself, sins by refusing to obey God (or even by refusing God, taking God's powers within the creature's power). Others, wanting to account for various problematics in the creature's world, find the sources of woe among the decisions made by ancient, not primitive, creatures. In one such account the creature's violence must be contained by blaming it upon some scapegoat, thus locating the foundation of culture in violence. Another locates it in the sexual passions of sons desiring to sleep with their mothers. The origin of civilization lies as it seeks to control such intrinsic behaviors. Commenting upon the rape of thousands of Tutsi women by Hutus, an observer states that the behavior lies just under the surface of each of us. In all these theologies or pseudo-theologies the result is the temptation to make culture—or even history—evil, an unsafe place for the creature, quite without resource to cope with the undeniably perilous situation.

With the world itself viewed not only as awe-full (a religious sensitivity) but consistently awful (the result of unfortunate theological definitions), the creature has little recourse except to have to continually defend God from its perennially unsatisfactory understanding of its world. Pastoral care is caught up in suffering and brokenness; personal, social, cultural, and international disasters; the melancholy or rage left over from unfulfilled expectations; and seeking always to explain and cure tragedies and horrors, unfairness and inequality. No wonder the creature resists claiming a creaturely stance, surrendering weakly or refusing violently.

And yet the experiences of the creatures also radiate with joy, sometimes even at deathbeds, and not infrequently in the lives of the disabled and chronically ill. Although Theodor Adorno (1997) is reported to have said that writing poetry after Auschwitz is barbaric, poetry continued to be written. Life goes on after deaths and despairs...Amy Lowell's nineteenth-century poem that "I forget just why" is only one level of response, as there are alternative theological themes to understand and care within the creature's context of mortality and other limitations.

These experiences, too, need to be accounted for. What God spoke of as good cannot be instantly transmuted into the negativities about history and culture that state much of contemporary theology's view of the world: broken and filled with violence. Western culture is viewed as imperialistic and materialistic; creatures are oppressed and invisible in their terror and suffering. It is a world where more creatures are seen to be claiming to be God than affirming the first duty of a religious person, that is, to state and feel deeply that the creature is *not* God.

This conversation about the creature's world continues through the essays. We are probing what it means to live with eye undimmed and bodily vitality undiminished this side of the promised land, or after the destruction of the temple, or through years of wandering in a wilderness. We ponder what it means to live in times such as these, with twenty-first–century issues of globalization and violence, radical pluralisms, and unanticipated developments in science and technology affecting and naming the creature's situation. Reflection on creatures experiencing chronic conditions of health and cultural situations may help us attend to these complex issues with somewhat new eyes— and clarify some of the particular skills and styles of presence sought after in pastoral care with creatures experiencing chronicity. There may be clues in the many worlds of chronicity as to how the creature can live with grace and even joy in such an outrageously terrible world!

Living with Chronicity

To live with chronicity is to live with a condition of long duration; or it may be something that is frequently recurring, a pattern over a long time, a handicapping condition or disability, Alzheimer's, a neurologically progressive disease. A state of chronicity is, of course, a state of limitation. It is a condition that doesn't get better or doesn't find restoration, such as Christopher Reeve's spinal cord injury or Michael J. Fox's diagnosis of Parkinson's. In many situations the condition may grow worse, as indeed, my own has. After living with the effects of polio for over forty years, the post-polio syndrome has caused deterioration in the muscle strength I had achieved, and that which had become strong through overcompensation has become weakness.

There may be good days and bad days, but the beloved with Alzheimer's continues to slip away from us and eat away at our caregiving energies (and finances). A person severely afflicted with cerebral palsy may make remarkable progress in communication with the help of a computer, but continues to lack bodily control and to be noticeable in a crowd and unintentionally disruptive in a classroom.

Being present with creatures who live in and with situations of chronicity preoccupies much pastoral time, but is seldom the subject of intentional theological reflection. How to understand chronicity is a primary theological issue. Unnoticed or unreflected on theological conclusions have affected personal and cultural views of creatures experiencing these kinds of limitations and hence have affected views of pastoral care. They demand recognizing bodily imperfection and disability of limb and mind, nervous and muscular systems, kidney failures and a variety of failures in hormonal production, and then placing their reality within God's goodness. The creature's genetic structure carries its own history of limitation and of unpredictability as to when one recessive gene and another recessive gene may meet.

But before we remind ourselves of the theological quagmires that have sought to make imperfect creatures invisible and an embarrassment to God and to other creatures, let us play the "what if" game that I used to play with my children. What if ice cream were served on top of spaghetti? What if the Chicago Cubs should win the World Series? What if persons living lives of chronicity—and their families—were positive models of whole human beings, that is, of creatures claiming their finitude and limitation, their creaturely stance, if you will, and receiving it with grace, perseverance, and continuing experiences of joy? What if their sense of the goodness of God was neither extinguished nor sentimentalized? And what if these claims and experiences did not mean giving up the creature's creativity and imagination in rightfully pushing the boundaries of finitude and limitation, and participating in a perennial process of discerning the differences among limitations imposed by creation, by history, by culture, and even by one's own family or religion?

Because of our fears and denials of death, we have lost sight of the ordinariness of death's passages amongst us. It is almost as if we had never noticed that everyone dies! When my husband and I served a small church as co-pastors we were asked by several in our primarily elderly congregation to preach on the meaning of death. Educated by psychologists of self-actualization and visionaries of social justice, this had simply never occurred to us. Nor did reflecting upon the chronic condition of kidney failure that accompanied the life (and death) of one of our few teenagers. I still recall the stark comment by the previously nonverbal father: "We never had no luck with our kids." And we have made of death a drama! And of chronicity a blessing or a curse. The magnificent writer Belden Lane (1991) describes his learnings in the many nursing home visits he made to his mother.

> When my mother's condition leveled out and even improved
> in certain ways I had to rethink the meaning I had sought

from her death. Her own acceptance of the delay in death's coming made me reconsider my restless impatience. No longer could I picture myself in tragic terms, defiantly confronting death, eager to get it over with as soon as possible. Instead, a more insistent question began to emerge. How would I cope with the uneventful, living from day to day in the absence of spectacular drama? How would I deal with *life*—a life that leans gently from death in the prolonged mystery of patience? (774)

Words such as "cope," "uneventful," "living from day to day," "living in the absence of spectacular drama," mark much of the daily living of those both engulfed and empowered in situations of chronicity. Lane speaks of the redundancy of ordinariness—the day-by-day plotting to get from bed to wheelchair to toilet to lunch, and the ordinary acts of helpfulness that some require in order for those everyday processes to go on. Lane wants a book called "When Ordinary Things Happen to Average People," and a "spirituality of the uneventful, of the places in one's life that are neither deep nor exhilaratingly high." Later we will look briefly at some particular people whose ordinary lives are made up of extraordinary effort to get dressed and be mobile, and who, with a slight shift in theological focus, we find as practitioners of the art of consenting to one's finitude and limitation while not surrendering one's creativity and compassion for others, or one's joy and trust in the goodness of God.

The Church's Worlds of Chronicity: A Brief and Sad History

Until very recently, the church had announced its theological stance about those with chronic conditions in its architecture. They couldn't get in; or, if they could, couldn't hear the words or see the hymns, had to sit in the back so their muscle spasms would not be noticeable. Likewise their helpers were instructed to keep them silent so as not to interrupt the holiness of the service. Even in my beloved church in Tennessee, I must sit in the back—in the flow of the air conditioner—as there is simply no suitable space elsewhere. As folks age, they may stay home because the bathrooms are not on the floors where the people are; if one gives birth to an infant with Down's syndrome or severe cerebral palsy, the public school system may be more receptive than the church.

The architecture states the traditional theology: The church is for perfect, and not imperfect, bodies—for imperfect bodies and minds disclose sin, or God's lack of power to prevent their occurrence. Since God is good, giving birth to an imperfect creature marks sinfulness, and the imperfect are to be invisible since they come too close to challenging the goodness of God or reminding us of the fragility of creaturehood and our susceptibility to flaws within our own genetic structure…and, hence, the failures of creation.

Thus, over the centuries imperfect bodies were abandoned or put away. In earlier periods of history, fine institutions were built to keep them in love and care, although abandoned by biological and ecclesial families. Even now persons experiencing the imperfections of the aging process are relegated to nursing home care; if they are poor or without medical insurance, they are cared for, appropriately enough, I suppose, by other poor folk, many without medical insurance. Our culture is one in which the chronic condition of aging has come to mean segregated housing, as has, of course, the chronic condition of being poor, or of a nonvalued social class. That this is the grounding of a theological point of view, only slowly changing, is clear in the historic understanding that persons with imperfect bodies cannot be ordained, as the ordained, representing God, must stand whole before God. The implications of this theology reside deeply within culture and community. If death and imperfection come into the world through sin, then giving birth to or growing into an imperfect body is a mark of one's sinful nature. With this "caused by sin" theology deeply embodied in culture, imperfect creatures were institutionalized or kept hidden at home. Since there was limited access up curbs and into buildings, finding bathrooms or traveling if the family did not have a car, the exclusions were supported by cultural practices, and denial of disability and other forms of chronicity (limitation) was supported by their absence. When I was a child there were still "freak shows" at carnivals, where for ten cents one could stare at the "freaks" of natural processes, abandoned, without companionship. Before hospice, many were abandoned by physicians and families to die alone in sterile hospitals. The power of the denial of death and disability has masked opportunities to care. Perhaps more important, it has prevented us from seeing the gifts of dying and disabled persons to our own understandings of creaturehood and a theology that in practices of pastoral care, caregiver and care receiver are one.

I want to make a theological point: the imperfect creature was an anomaly to the goodness of God. The *imago dei* was not for every creature. Those with chronic conditions who did not get better were viewed as failures of medical science or prayer life. But they simply disclosed the biochemical, genetic composition of human creatures, their accidents and their essences, their claims to be God (forgetting the woundedness and signs of disability in the hands and feet of their Savior), and their refusals to claim and consent to their position in the world as creatures, subject to genetic, virus, chemical peril. Theologically, such creatures have seemed to be an embarrassment to God who still seems to need defense against chronicity. The defense becomes progressively harder to make, recognizing, as we do, that most creatures will be composed of some genetic, chemical, biological condition that will state their finitude and limitation whether or not they claim it. And deep inside the creatures' hearts lie the sense of being punished if an imperfect child is born (why me?) or if one experiences diabetes, mental illness, or forgetfulness. In a recent classroom conversation a student said, "I guess we're just cursed to live within our genes!"

But what if? What if Christopher Reeve, before his death, embodied a positive model for receiving the slings and arrows of outrageous fortune by refusing cynicism or surrender, and instead, blessed with resources, lifted up hope for all with spinal injuries and organized commitment for major research in the area of spinal cord injuries? What if Jim, whose story we will read later, lifts up the persistence of having to take three hours to deal with his bowels and his dressing in the morning before he can leave the house as a positive quality of endurance and faithfulness? What if we can learn from those with chronic conditions something of how to consent to finitude and limitation without surrendering to being of less value and living without joy or hope? What if chronicity is closer to being a paradigm of humanity than the self aware and autonomous human person?

Chronicity and the Cultures of Care

As Belden Lane observes his mother's bone cancer and later slide into Alzheimer's, he notes how uneventful and commonplace chronic illness and dying processes are. Instead of a drama of fighting death, or conquering illness, he views a passage through the mundane, with wheelchairs and diapers, the effort of conversation and the presence of many partners in his mother's everyday care.

Situations of chronic illness or disability are varied; family responses differ, as does the participation of the involved creature. A student told the story of Jim, determined after he lost a leg to be the best possible one-legged man and athlete. A second accident left him a paraplegic, daily having to attend to his bowels and invest hours into making it possible to be mobile. One of my students, Cindy, sits rigid in a wheelchair or stands rigid at a desk. She requires a full-time attendant and her twisted arms and feet are not hidden. This woman with a law degree and a passion for theological education requires a full-time attendant to move with her through the ordinary activities of a day. She notes that when people first see her they may not see a lawyer or a theologian, but someone to be pitied, in need of full-time care. Yet her Christmas letter, reporting on further bodily deterioration and technological dependence, also reported a number of events "which have boldly evidenced God's direct and ongoing presence in [her] life."

Many persons experiencing chronic illnesses or disabilities are dependent upon caring helpers, some of them described in a recent *New York Times* article as "the invisible women who fan out across the city each day, mostly traveling by subway, to go into people's homes and do the grunt work of caring for those who are sick or infirm." The column, by Bob Herbert (2002), goes on to describe one particular culture of care:

> There are thousands of home health aides in New York City and they work hard, taking on the tasks that most people, even close relatives, shun. "We bathe the clients, and feed them and dress them and give them their medication," said Mary Toni, "We run errands and take them to their doctors' appointments. Whatever is necessary, that's what we do."

A large group of caring partners are such women and men, not only in home health care, but in nursing homes and residential treatment centers, short term hospital facilities for the care of severely mentally-ill persons, and in hospital facilities as licensed practical nurses. We are saying two things. First, such acts of care are vital to the person's dignity and to the humane character of a culture. Invisible, like many chronically ill persons themselves, they witness to a culture's refusal of the importance of ordinary care, and to the value of little kindnesses, ordinary touch by persons who are not repelled by disfigured bodies, and presences that co-create a relational world even within the limited worlds that physical disabilities may define; for they are not culturally valued, with affirmation and/or a living wage. Ultimately as every death is local, so, too, is every person with a chronic condition. To be accompanied *in that condition* is pastoral care as sure as the care of the physician or psychiatrist, surgeon, rabbi, or priest.

Second, those who attend the ordinary needs of persons whose bodies are different receive the lowest wages in our culture. Many of them carry no health insurance, are dependent upon public transportation, have trouble supporting their families. As we have seen, the creature is finite and limited, historical and situated; the creature is also relational as a part of creation. Many persons with chronic disabilities are blessed by the relational ties of a loving family. Many others' relational needs are met—if at all—by underpaid attendants. Perhaps the latter are those within the many cultures of care to be the most affirmed—and well paid.

Our historical period may prefer big metaphors: fighting death and extending life expectancy; eliminating poverty and violence; creating inclusive communities; and eradicating terrorism. Even as we pledge ourselves to these tasks, we must attend to the particular, tending to the entirely beautiful creatures that live within and behind the metaphors and goals of a people. For to embody the care and community that God intends is the task and not the given. The present task may be to be joyfully in the presence of a severely deformed body, with major communication problems, saliva escaping from the mouth, unable to feed oneself, dependent on others in the areas of dress, elimination, and sexual activity…and find there a colleague in ministry, coming to seminary partly to witness to his wholeness, and to teach others. May this be an epitaph for David Morton, who shared his life and his needs with the Eden Seminary community—as full partner—for five years.

Charles Gerkin (1979, 1984, 1986, 1991, 1997) is one of the contemporary fathers of pastoral care. He views the human situation as one of unlimited aspiration and finite possibility. The gift of the severely disabled to human community may be to hold this in continuing tension, engaging their possibilities and limitations in ways that model the situation of all human creatures. From the margins the disabled, the persons with handicapping conditions, those with illnesses that don't get better…speak and witness that, in this case, the margins become the center, as all of us die, run into our particular facts of glass, experience chronicity, and learn how to live this side of the promised land. Perhaps they will make the best witnesses to pastoral care as witnessing to joy and the goodness of God.

Toward a Nuanced Theology

The question of such folk as David and Cindy shifts from "*why me?*"—Why Did God do this to my body…do this to *me?*—to affirming that this body *is* me. David and I only knew David in his particular body, created in and embodying the Image of God as it was given. In learning that bodies die, we find more time and value for palliative care, and for intentional human community through the processes of dying, refusing abandonment and the fears of mortality as intrinsic. We study, teach about, and experience death and chronicity as integral to creation, and dying and chronically disabled creatures as indeed entirely beautiful! And there are, after all, more of us than of the other kind!

A theology that is suspicious of science and technology must also look to what technological advance means to persons who can become full participants in human community, including the work force, through computer technologies. Christopher Reeve devoted his body and resources to lessen the devastating results of spinal cord injuries, and Michael J. Fox envisions better care of those with Parkinson's. The boundaries are pushed, even as the boundary situation is received without cynicism or withdrawal.

Theologically, our understanding of grace is frequently limited to special grace, which heals and cures, blesses with bright lights and clarity. But there is also ordinary grace, which hugs us quietly, helps to make an impossible moment possible to get through, nurtures the sense of one's own beauty in a body that the unperceptive dismiss as ugly...or punishment. Theologically, God is not only good when our lives go well.

If death and disability come into the world through sin, then we can be falsely sentimental about how bravely persons bear their conditions; how severe disablement can be a blessing, and, after all, one wouldn't have the condition unless God knew that one could deal with it. These are the responses of a non-nuanced theology that seeks to apply a theological principle to particular historical situations. But creation carries its own elements into human form and surrounds and penetrates this form with its many energies. The creature is, to be sure, mortal and limited, but shares in these same forces. As the world nurturing and surrounding it, the creature consists of creative and imaginative energies, responds to caring presences, shares a common vulnerability with others, and, in that recognition, at least sometimes finds the joys of companionship as well as the grief of not being in control, of not being God. As we shall see, neurotic needs for control and time management are one of the dynamics that get in the way of the creature's capacity to experience joy— thus my suggestion that those with chronic conditions might bear witness to an alternative understanding of human wholeness.

As Henri Nouwen found his life in a community of persons with disabilities, perhaps the formation of some alternative communities could be those who have found ways to consent to their condition while still stretching boundaries and finding joy and goodness. And instead of bumper stickers that proclaim "shit happens," we might find some ways to state that creation is rich in energies of both brute and gentle force. I like Meland's phrase myself: "All existing places where ultimacy and immediacy traffic together and can celebrate is brought with peril as well as with possibility and promise" (Meland 1976, 45). Both Meland's thought and pastoral care situations seek to place ultimacy and immediacy in the same sentence where they traffic together in the depth of the creature's ordinary living.

Crisis

UNFOLDINGS AND INTRUSIONS

Some philosophers have described the creature as being thrown into existence. This is probably an apt phrase for some dimensions of the crisis experience. Suddenly—out of the blue—a self-evident or taken for granted situation is shattered. Planes fly into the World Trade Center. The eagerly awaited child arrives as a stillbirth. The dreaded phone call tells of a traffic death, or the knock on the door brings news of a beloved's death from a sudden heart attack. The creature feels thrown into an unfamiliar place without the previous resources. These are strange and chaotic times to be lived through, probably followed by in-between or out of place times until a new structure is slowly formulated. The new structure cannot be a replication of the old. There are different people, a different time, and the one affected by the crisis is a different person.

The creature is vulnerable to such intrusions into what was expected to be safe and secure. The intrusion may be terrorists, or forces of nature: tornadoes, floods, forest fires. The intrusion may be caused by bodily decrepitude or another person's decision. The intrusion may be a crash of a plane that one wasn't supposed to be on, or a carjacking in a suburban mall parking lot. There is nothing that can end the risk of sudden death or a birth anomaly. Crisis is but another form of the creature's perennially perilous situation, another form of recognition of lack of control, of being creature and not God.

A crisis may also appear as the unfolding of a normal developmental sequence. Used to the sweetness of some one year olds, a momentary crisis may occur as some two year olds momentarily undercut parental confidence and home arrangements. Adolescence may be a time of crisis in the formation of identity, with biological forces shattering some serenity and stating new feelings. In some cultures such developmental crises are ritualized; thrown into liminal space in between childhood and adulthood, the culture may provide a series of experiences and a ritual guide to assist the process of moving from one structure toward another. In such cultures the guide knows where the journey should end.

An institution may experience a crisis as its services are found wanting by a new generation, a new set of public issues, a new neighborhood demographics. And institutions, like creatures, may resist change and be unable to offer clear guidance to the creatures they seek to serve.

Crisis as Unavoidable

Whether intrusive or unfolding, the creature's life and culture are shaped by crises and responses to it. The author Stephen King spoke of the randomness of things when he reflected upon the death of the driver who hit him, leaving him with a leg broken in nine places, a split knee, and a fractured hip among other injuries. His life and that of the driver came together in a strange way, almost as a force of nature. Perhaps my own husband's heart muscle failed because of an electrical failure in his bodily system, a genetic defect, a built-in limitation on his life span. In an instant he was gone, and I was thrown into the chaos of having lost a husband, best friend, and person who loved my disabled body. Indeed many crises are of coincidence, random occurrences, unintended consequences of other actions, or lying resident within the creature's body. Recently a future Olympic figure skater was found dead in his bed, having previously had excellent medical exams and care. Of course, some crises are caused by intentional acts, like a spouse's suddenly leaving a marriage. The crises engendered by intentional acts of cruelty deserve special treatment; we will consider them in the next essay.

A person, institution, or even a culture may consider itself to be safe from crisis. A dear friend who never smoked is diagnosed with lung cancer. A faithful congregation faces budgetary crisis as its members age and there are no new younger members to take their places. A culture—the United States of America—may face a crisis of self-knowledge and self-definition when it experiences itself as not safe from the intrusion of violence. In the presence of crisis, the affected ones may first seek to secure themselves. Like the shock of suddenly perceiving one's finitude and limitation, one may turn backward, seeking restoration of what was. One may enter into the new with resistance and cynicism, seeking to place blame for what has occurred. We will later see how choosing closure may offer only illusory safety, and probably will cut one off from any future experiences of joy and goodness. The widow may shut herself off from her friends. The survivors may continue to live off the energy of rage—and carry it into the next generation. The care offered during a crisis is crucial to the future. The care offered during the period of moving, however slowly, to a new place of stability may be determinative of the individual or institution's future capacities to receive or offer care.

One form of care is participating in the formation of creatures who are grounded enough to be able to move through transitional liminal times without the neurotic need for premature closure or the pathological need to place blame. It is important to remember that crisis forces response—if there is death, there must be a funeral; if there is diagnosis, there must be treatment, or at least a decision about it; if there is flooding in the office buildings of downtown Houston, the water damage must be repaired; if buildings have been caused to collapse in lower Manhattan, the debris must be removed and, eventually, the possibilities of redevelopment can be imagined and negotiated, fought over and implemented.

The Caring Partnerships of Calamity

The discipline of pastoral care has not normatively included disaster ministries in its various programs. This witnesses to a singular focus upon therapy and professionalism. Now there is the need for congregations and their leaders to be aware of the many partners that deal with disaster. Without expanding on this, the responses to the disasters of September 11 were attended to by thousands of caregivers. The pastoral care focus was on opening churches for prayer and cries of lament, for gathering with others uncertain what to do or what to say, for lifting up in ritual experiences consolation and hope and, while listening to voices of rage and anger, refusing cries for retribution.

Responses to devastating hurricanes find many of the same partners, with various primary concerns for basic services, followed by repair crews and psychological services. At times of flood, churches may become centers of food preparation and shelter, and may liaison with other partners to find ways to focus resources of the many who want to help. Churches may hold candlelight services following the murder or horrendous death of a child. Hopefully the caregivers will carry some theological perspectives that neither seek to explain away nor prematurely comfort. Most important is their presence, their participation in the shared vulnerability of the creature. There comes a time for letting go, both of expectations and possessions, then of persons who are no longer there. As we can learn about a creaturely stance from persons experiencing situations of chronicity, we can learn about what it means that life goes on from those who live through crisis with new—or even continuing—faithfulness and hope.

Situations of crisis state very clearly the need for partnerships of care. Many laypersons serve on rescue teams and ambulance crews. Persons in the military, police departments, and fire departments may be unequally distributed among congregations, depending upon economic status. This is even more the situation with those who care for persons with severe chronic conditions. Their voices are frequently not present in committees developing mission statements or establishing programs of lay education for pastoral care. Yet they carry the burdens of ordinary care for church and culture.

Life Goes On

After the crisis event, a series of processes occur in liminal time. Pastoral care modes of guidance may be helpful here, although some crises may find the ordained leadership as uncertain of the way as the most ordinary layperson. The community affected needs to gather and reflect. Eventually the processes create new forms and under-standings, connections with the old and anticipations of the new. It is recorded that after the great flood, Noah planted a vine, made wine, and got drunk. On September 11, 2002, the one-year anniversary of those tragic events, an entire country remembered, began to plan for what might best fill the empty spaces in lower

Manhattan, and watched the children of absent fathers celebrate their birthdays. Life had gone on. There is a resiliency in creatures and their cultures.

After Auschwitz life went on, former inhabitants of the "Death Camps" gathered to Praise God. The floodwaters recede, and after some time has passed a small community on the Mississippi River finds that in its resettlements it has lost its history and its residential community. There are many possible variations. Sometimes crisis happens and nobody seems to notice, as well stated in the Auden poem, "Musee des Beaux Arts":

> About suffering they were never wrong,
> The Old Masters, how well they understood
> Its human position, how it takes place
> While someone else is eating or opening a
> Window or just walking dully along.
> …even the dreadful martyrdom must run its course
> anyhow in a corner, some untidy spot
> where the dogs go on with their doggy life
> and the torturer's horse
> scratches its innocent behind on a tree.
> In Brueghel's Icarus for instance, how everything
>   turns away quite leisurely from the
> disaster, the ploughman may have heard the
>   splash, the forsaken cry,
> but for him it was not an important failure; the sun shone
> as it had to go on the white legs disappearing into the green
> water, and the expensive delicate ship that must have seen
> something amazing, a boy falling out of the sky,
> had somewhere to get to and sailed calmly on.
>   (W. H. Auden, 1991, 179)

I felt publicly marked by my crisis; my husband was dead. I had no one to cook supper for. I had no arms to lie in, no presence with me while watching sports on TV. But the world went on around me; no one outside my family or acquaintances even knew that my world had been shattered. Similarly, when we watch crisis events on TV we are unaware that the crisis is not affecting the whole world. During the riots on the streets of Chicago, shown in horror on TV, I drove through those streets each day on my way to work, right at the edge of the violence. In urban culture, thousands of inner-city young men may be falling away, with nobody seeming to notice. Pastoral care needs eyes to see such future disasters, and ears to hear the cries of the afflicted. In the summer heat, even today, abandoned elderly persons, without air conditioning, die alone in their stifling apartments. After a tornado, the "poor folk" in the devastated community (in the trailer parks) often experience a disproportionate amount of the damage. Pastoral care needs eyes and ears and connections with churches that do not normatively participate in ecumenical dialogue for help in the seeing and hearing, as well as in finding authentic access to those who suffer.

Crisis may also set the stage for the next crisis! A crisis in dilapidated housing may motivate those who care to build new public housing, which may so isolate the residents that in several decades the solution to one crisis has itself become a crisis. The present crisis of a shortage of affordable housing may support the theory that housing for poor persons is a chronic situation. The crisis of the death of a young child may lead to a crisis in the marriage of the parents. A crisis of sexual abuse by a priest or pastor may lead to other crises, including those of authority and public embarrassment for the institution—even to a crisis of faith in those caught off guard by the occurrence.

It is probable that every historical period and situated community is affected by the peculiar set of contemporary issues that lead to crises as communities variously seek to encounter them. The issue of pluralism creates crises as congregations decide whom God wants them to include, and as nations determine fault and punishment for acts of terrorism or anticipated terrorism. Globalization states issues of economic crises, which affect drivers who must pay more for gas, and ordinary workers in small towns whose former employers have moved to other countries. New developments in science and technology state crises in ethical decision making, and acts of violence and the pervasiveness of evil state crisis issues of prevention and control, punishment and retaliation, civil liberties and public duties to protect citizens. If pastoral care is to bear witness to joy and the goodness of God, it must also bear with its beloved creatures as they ponder their perilousness and seek groundings that hold them together—and call them to celebration!

Crisis, Culture, and Pastoral Care

Creatures living after crisis may sing along with Bruce Springsteen, "tell me how do you live brokenhearted" ("Mary's Place" on *The Rising*, Sony, 2002). This is a central theological issue in pastoral care, raised by the creature's perilous and perennial situation as finite, limited, historically situated…and subject to the vulnerabilities of chronic illness and conditions, crisis and the presence of evil and violence in the world.

Cultural crises may shift from generation to generation. That is, my generation's participation in the cruelties of the Second World War is forgotten. Those who participated in and protested against the war in Vietnam are aging, and my students now pray about the war in Iraq, about the crises among the religious siblings with divergent claims to Jerusalem, about how to preach on future September 11s. Even here, crisis provides the unchosen opportunity for reflection and critique, for conversation about values and goals. Within the discipline of pastoral care, family systems practitioners note the potential for positive change through a family crisis, especially when participants in the system can be teased or eased into dialogue, when one member can make changes that affects the whole, or where there is a leadership style of non-anxious presence that can help to free the system to be responsible in caring better for itself.

The responses to personal, family, congregational, and cultural crises are not that different. Theologically the agonized cries of the creatures are to be listened to. Following the disasters in Oklahoma City and lower Manhattan the churches, synagogues, and mosques were opened for prayer and, hopefully, some comforting presence. Listening remains a radical requirement for caring processes to unfold without premature attempts to fix things or take action (revenge or other premature moves such as a widower moving out of his house) or offer hope as if it were a commodity instead of a trusting orientation.

There are rituals and the statements of comfort, meaning, and direction that they offer, often to folk who are surprised by their efficacy. Following September 11 most public rituals were not only ecumenical but also interfaith, the ritual itself making a statement about the common vulnerabilities of the creatures: mortal, guilty, yet entirely beautiful. As time passed a variety of guides sought to offer direction, corporately religious leaders counseled against retaliation while recognizing the horrendous evil. Hopefully survivors received care and guides in their own places of worship and faith traditions, learning how to live brokenhearted, consenting to what it means to be finite, gradually able to envision an ongoing life. By September 11, 2002, debris had been hauled away and various community leaders were ready to begin fighting about what should be built on the empty land.

For life does go on. There are many religious metaphors that state the need for certain faithful qualities through desert wanderings, family separations, and murder of one's leader. Endurance and persistence may some days top the list…just getting by, a day at a time. On other days one may be able to experience gratitude for the gifts that yet hold one in existence, the first birthday parties of children whose fathers were killed, nurturing communities, new friendships forged out of searing pain, wrought out of interior battles between hopelessness and hope. Some may carry the terrors forever within them, all cures failing, but with understandings of care a nonperishable presence.

Theologically living through crisis models both the transiency and the continuity of the creature's world, where containers of meaning crack but are repaired before all of the water of life has drained away.

And in the midst of crisis the creature may experience, and hence come to know, the reality of Spirit and presence of God that is as truly located in the depths and textures of everyday existence as in the more amorphous mists of heavy or abstract principles which are supposed to frame the meaning of existence. Anna Quindlen (2002) wrote a column on September 11, 2002, which claims that date as also marking the joyful event of her son's birthday. Both events are real. Both permeate the meaning she places on cultural and personal existence.

As we have discussed crisis we have edged into conversation about a world of evil and violence, terrorism and intentional cruelty, which must be encountered before we dare to speak with confidence of joy and the goodness of God.

Deliver Us from Evil

Violence, Evil and Acts of Terrorism

Perhaps the greatest shock of finitude is to be the recipient of intentional acts of violence. The various responses to the terrorist attacks on September 11, 2001, are informing. In the United States it is as if there has been a sudden discovery that this is a frightening world in which even God's "favored" creatures are vulnerable to horrors. It is as if a nation discovers what is old stuff to other nations and geographic areas. For, as commentators generally agree, the twentieth century has been filled with human acts of violence against other humans: massacres and suicide bombers; concentration camps and torture; withholding of food and shelter and unconcern over the breakup of families; and the catastrophic situations of abandoned children, raped women, mutilated men.

As we move toward conversations about pastoral care in such a context, I have been helped to see its starkness through the eyes and metaphors of several current participant observers.

Miroslav Volf, a native of what used to be a part of Yugoslavia, speaks of contemporary culture as drenched in evil. He defines the exclusions that allow human beings to make others anonymous, invisible, and in other ways less than human so that they might be annihilated or oppressed. Yet in the midst of this dreadful cacophony of evil, he insists that Christians can and must reach out to embrace, to see others and make possible human community. His argument for nonviolence is, however, complex and penetrating, and his call for action demanding. I find it helpful to reflect on a statement made by Professor Meland when I studied with him in the late '50s. He had just returned from sabbatical study in India and was pondering the radically different religious and cultural experiences that he had encountered. He asked us to enter into a brooding style of inquiry on the phrase: "Love one another we must, but let no one underestimate the difficulties of the task." I continue to ponder that even as I reflect on what I understand to be Volf's clearest statement:

> My thesis that the practice of non-violence requires a belief in divine vengeance will be unpopular with many Christians, especially theologians in the West. To the person who is inclined to dismiss it, I suggest imagining that you are delivering a lecture in a war zone (which is where a paper that underlies this chapter was originally delivered). Among your listeners are people whose cities and villages have been first plundered, then burned, and leveled to the ground, whose daughters and sisters have been raped; whose fathers and brothers have had their throats slit. The topic of the lecture: a Christian attitude toward violence. The thesis: we should not retaliate since God is perfect non-coercive love. Soon you would discover that it takes the quiet of a suburban home for the birth of the thesis that human non-violence corresponds to God's refusal to judge. In a scorched land, soaked in the blood of the innocent, it will invariably die. And as one watches it die, one will do well to reflect about many other pleasant captivities of the liberal mind. (1996, 304)

As you can tell, Volf speaks out of a culture that has experienced violence historically and in the present moment. Situations such as this are not the ordinary context of the North American church: Intentional violence experienced in Oklahoma City and lower Manhattan has perhaps shifted a style of religious thinking that made America God's promised land and filled us with the certainties of blessing and security. The brutalities of the Civil War have, of course, been forgotten even while memories of master/slave relationships live on along with the purchase of bodies and the breakup of families. The presence of hidden evils within this culture is too familiar to be described here. What is important is what this means to conversations about care as the dynamics of the twenty-first century unfold to shape the context and define the situations in which we finite, historical, limited, mortal, guilty, and entirely beautiful creatures are to care for one another. How are we to learn to understand one another over time in sufficient depth and respect that the solution of killing one another is no way out?

Others than Volf are helpful in clarifying this particular context of care, where the shock of one's finite situation is experienced through what seem to be gratuitous acts of violence. I focus on evil as intentional, or as emerging out of such total self-regard that its victims are not even seen. Invisible, their personal dignity can be violated or destroyed. This calls forth, for some of us, long-forgotten arguments about the devil and the rapture. Harvey Cox is clear that violence is inescapable and always has been. What has been lost in modernity is a language of evil, devil, apocalypticism. A chaplain friend in a children's hospital frequently dealing with the results of the violence of abuse in its caring practices reported on his staff's resistance to the word *evil* as "too primitive." Cox argues that childish innocence about the continuing presence of violence in even a postmodern world must be put aside in favor of the adult version of the world, which includes violence and evil within it. The issues are not those of primitive versus modern or postmodern creatures, but of the perennial persistence of violence and evil in creation itself.

This experience of the shock of finitude may be even harder to absorb than the shock of realizing that one will die, or live with a progressive disease that gradually paralyzes one's body or takes away that which has sustained one through an unexpected crisis. Since practices of care are also particular to different cultures, care in the United States must attend to the loss of the expectation of America as an elect nation. Mark Slouka (2002) ponders the ramifications of the attack of September 11 being "not just a terrorist attack. This was an act of metaphysical trespass." By that he means the loss of the myth of American exceptionalism, "the world-redeeming ark of Christ, chosen, above all the nations of the world, for a special dispensation."

He presents a case for both the personal, and deeply theological, issues:

When I wondered aloud to another acquaintance how it was possible for a man's faith to sail over Auschwitz, say, only to founder on the World Trade Center, I found myself quickly taken to task for both my myopia and my callousness—the product, he implied, of my excessively European sensibility. He himself had been in a state of crisis for two months, he said. He slept badly, struggled with depression. His children were afraid to get in the subway or walk past a tall building, and there was nothing he could tell them. He was considering leaving New York and moving to Mexico. "How can you not see that everything is different now?" he concluded. "And anyway, who are you to decide when it's right for someone to have a crisis of faith?" (37–38)

Slouka's ponderings are directly related to our ponderings. "For I did not believe that everything was different now. A horrible thing occurred, and all affected by the tragedy deserve and deserved compassion—as, he suggested, those who lost a teenager killed in a traffic accident the afternoon of the eleventh." But he goes on, "This was not London during the Blitz. Or Stalingrad in the winter of 1943. Or Sarajevo in 1994. Thousands of innocent people had died, true. But innocents had been dying for a while now—millions of them, mostly children, as quietly as melting snow each and every year."

I share this as a reminder of the persistence of violence and evil in the world, with creatures reflecting upon it even as they have experienced its horrors from the very beginnings. Built into the fabric of Hebrew-Christian reflections is the story of Cain and Abel, and the Old Testament is filled with texts of terror and violations of dignity. The Christian affirmation of hope (resurrection) arises (literally) out of a violent act and, as contemporary history reminds us once again, all religions carry within them a shadow side of violence. I myself have come to believe that the more certain you are in your knowledge of God—coupled with your certainty about what God wants from other creatures—the more dangerous you are and the more you perpetuate the violence in the world that, in my theology, begins with the creatures' refusal to be creature, created and not God, not the Creator. The first duty of creature is to confess not to be God.

But Slouka's other reflection is also relevant to understanding pastoral care in relation to the shock of receiving the news that one is finite, limited, and not God. That is the persistent narcissism in which an individual, or a family, or a tribe, or a nation, only notices horrendous evils if they are experienced by oneself…or those who are extensions of one's own self. Slouka wondered where his friend had been hiding when "half a million human beings were being massacred in Rwanda, not a few of them in churches." His crisis of faith did not materialize until the evil act of violence was massive (not a hit-and-run drunk driver) and close to home (not in far away lands with tribal peoples). I wonder about the privileged escape my beloved country has had from being infected by the genealogies of hatred and retribution that are carried over generations or centuries. Out of the old stories of being competitors for land and power, domination and being God's favorite, even the children of the one God of all kill one another through violence and disdain.

The Contributions of Feminism

In this country pastoral care entered the dialogue about violence and evil quite late, not around issues of slavery and labor unions, dangerous public housing or other issues of poverty, but, understandably and rightfully so, around issues of the rape and sexual abuse of women. As the voices of women began to speak of clergy misuse of power in relation to their parishioners or students, one form of issues of violence and abuse was brought into mainstream pastoral care and counseling conversations. Men, of course, joined the dialogue, and some of the vital contributions shifted the conversation from issues of sexuality to issues of power; from silence and secrecy to sharing and exposing practices buried deeply within institutional, cultural, and theological expressions themselves. Attempts at prevention and care emerged. Through training and education, and the intentional creation of comfortable, safe, and secure places where stories could be shared and where shared sufferers could gather together for support and affirmation, the new embodiment of cure of souls offered solicitous concern along with empowerment and liberation. The intentional creation of rituals and theological perspectives that challenged unrecognized violence within familiar structures was both nurturing and offered resistance to words and worldviews that were hurtful. Alerts to the pervasiveness of violence and evil in a world of domination and oppression, secrecy and denial, were written and spoken about, although too often these were perceived as feminist issues. The growing number of minority persons within professional conversations added concern for the violence that attends racism and homophobia.

While the provision of care included counseling and therapeutic interventions seeking a shift from victim imagery to survivor and full participant images, the reality of violence and evil was not trivialized to make it subject to therapy, to protocols of recovery—to cure, if you will. Yet the vestiges of a therapeutic mentality persevere in conversations about violence, evil, and acts of terrorism. At some levels they are helpful—even as they raise issues of greater complexity. As we move toward some theological understandings of the origins of evil and the prevalence of violence in the creature's world, we begin with a statement from the Psychoanalytic Institute in St. Louis, Missouri:

> We try to understand why people would decide to end their life in order to take another's. I doubt that any of us in St. Louis have treated political terrorists, but certainly psychoanalytic concepts can help us understand the mind of the terrorist. The person who has done the most work in this area is Dr. Jerrold Post at George Washington University. He has worked with the CIA for over 20 years. He has interviewed more than 100 Middle East terrorists and applied psychoanalytic ideas in trying to understand the dynamics of these individuals. Basically what happens is that charismatic destructiveness ends up replacing what we would think of as conscience in narcissistically vulnerable individuals. These people believe that they are trying to live toward a greater ideal that is beyond themselves. They view themselves as martyrs for a cause. I think it is important that we understand that this is their perspective. It is not just that these are evil destructive people. Some may well be, but this is too easy. It doesn't mean we shouldn't try to stop them or prosecute them. It does mean that if we can try to understand the phenomena, we might be able to do something about it. The ability of a group to

perceive another group as all bad while their own group is seen as all good is characteristic of much group behavior. We experience this in play at football games. However, when it crosses a line, it becomes quite destructive. In terms of trying to understand these phenomena, we need a broad perspective.

What might such a perspective include?

Evil: Inside, Outside, or All around the Block?

Some interpreters of modernity and persons standing within an optimistic therapeutic tradition tend to view evil as forces that come from outside the creature. The prevailing wisdom would be that evil has nothing to do with human nature and is rather attributed to political institutions. Thus institutions and cultures swamp, so to speak, the inherent goodness of the creature. Culture itself becomes evil; grounded in violence, the history of culture is one of "scapegoating," states Baillie, and there is no escape except the Christian cross. For others there is a history of monsters residing with human beings, with only a thin layer protecting us from our own negative vitalities. Certainly the prominence of murder mysteries on best-seller lists attests to this. P. D. James, one of my favorites, states it better than many theorists: "and now…there was this murder, bloody, obscene, with its overtones of madness and revenge, to demonstrate how fragile was that elegant, complicated bridge of order and reason which the law had constructed down the centuries over the abyss of social and psychological chaos."

Frequently caught in-between references to the ways in which toddlers pound on each other and adolescents turn into terrorists on islands that are given them for development (as in *Lord of the Flies*), the issue has been carried within pastoral care in terms of personality theory. When asked, "Why Doesn't the Kingdom Come?" theologian Peter Hodgson (1972) referred to the creature's dynamics psycho-logically understood. It cannot come because of interior conflict at such great depth nothing can transform it. Or, while the technologies of change are available, so that humans could be shaped to live in Walden II, if not utopia, we refuse these gifts of science and technology. Or institutions so weigh down the human potential for growth and for good that progress is stymied and possibility denied. That God's kingdom might already have come in gentle defiance of cruelty and terror, and that insistence upon relationships of equality and equal regard are what make it visible, is a disappointing thought. For, as the song goes, "Is That All There Is?" Marjorie Suchocki (1988) views the "background cacophony of evil" as permeating institutions, communities, nations, whole epochs. It is sustained by "a multiply nuanced and mirrored and repeated intentionality of purpose that exercises its corporate influence." This is, as she puts it, the low intensity evil of the ways "things work" or the way "things simply are," the exclusionary vapors of institutional or communal cultures under which many suffer but for which no one is responsible and about which all complain but no one can target. This all-pervasive low intensity evil rejuvenates itself by engendering belief in its own immortality and imposes itself by generating a sense of its own ineluctability.

Such sophisticated and intangible practices can lead those who most decry violence against the poor to participate in the exclusionary practice of tenure, while driving new model cars, living in upscale houses, sending their children to private schools, and grading their students on the proper interpretation of scripture as God favoring the poor. I find that my own interpretations go both ways. On the one hand, I regret the loss of Eden, and sin coming into the world in a way that makes human creatures responsible for it. For, if that were not the case, it would become God's fault, and the history of theology has been one of creating arguments by excusing acts of horrendous evil, pernicious violence, and unredeemable victims by placing the burden upon the shoulders of creatures who make bad decisions, seek to secure themselves by destroying others, or, among other things, refusing to concede that they are not God.

But on the other hand, I resent conservatives and liberals alike who would create utopias and organize, through law or revolution, to make their vision of human community an historic possibility. Out of such desires for the good of their "fellow man" can arise unimaginable cruelties of war and the creation of narratives for those who hold the wrong point of view that set in motion more antagonistic narratives that are carried throughout history.

Paul Pruyser (1976) states that the human creature likes to "deny the reality status of unpleasant things." Certainly the reality of violence and evil falls into this category, even more, probably, than the denial of death, chronicity, and the chaos that follows crisis. A variety of perspectives can guide us in our practices of care. If the culture itself is evil, and suffering is the only authentic response of the creature in its world, the practice of care cannot count on cultural resources—or the joys and delights of creaturehood are viewed as too puny to matter. Or the situation may be understood as one of tragedy, not sin, where horrendous evils are not explained, but, rather, God's compassion is present with and within them. This type of interpretation allows for categories of valuing the creature's persistence, resistance of evil in its own place, and celebration as it receives compassion from Creator God and the other creatures who share the same boat.

For others, failures to hear or see another are carried deep within the orbits of meaning that we referred to earlier, their effects having an influence on present relationships. These "surds of insensitivity" do not, however stand alone. They are always in the presence of the depths of love also carried within historical process, where gentle might stands always opposed to brute force. And, at some point, confronted with brute reality and gentle might, the creatures choose. Pruyser would hope that they would choose the forces of benevolence over those of malevolence, both authentic and a dimension of creaturely existence, or, if not choose between them, that the creature lives between belief and unbelief, between benevolence and malevolence, between promised visions and experience historical realities.

Some Practices of Care in the Midst of Violence/Evil

If violence is dependent upon anonymous faces and invisible others, then one small act is the embodiment of pastoral care practices of seeing faces and listening to all creatures. Care seeks embrace, the embrace of difference and hence the embrace of the possibility of community. For pastoral persons who feel distant from the forces of the world within abstract dynamics of globalization, pluralism, and terrorism, the practice of particularity, embrace, and little kindnesses in one's own places is an act of resistance.

I grew up with the three monkeys (hear no evil, see no evil, speak no evil) on my grandmother's desk and my parents' bookcase These monkeys serve to perpetuate violence as they encourage the keeping of secrets and the pretense that one does not see what is going on.

Such refusals catch participants in the banalities of evil…by not seeing, hearing, and speaking, we unintentionally support violent practices.

Following the events of terrorism in Oklahoma City and lower Manhattan, pastoral caregivers responded by opening churches, providing places for the expression of feeling (often anger and rage), offering the presence of others with whom to cry and grieve. There are times when the touch of another gets one through impossible times. The events of September 11, 2001, led to focusing more on analysis and theological offerings as to where God was, issues of retribution, ponderings of the presence of violence in the culture of the victims, and celebration of the many caregivers who put their bodies on the line in response. Reflection on these events of violence, evil, and terrorism leads to some valued qualities of the creaturely stance that might be more intentionally invited in the practices of care: resilience, persistence, resistance, endurance, the capacity not to let one's own narcissism affect the understanding of an event. I doubt that pastoral care as an educational modality had sponsored any pre-September 11 reflections on the shock of finitude, the persistence of evil in the world, an analysis of evil and violence present in immediate situations, or the wisdom that creatures have their hearts broken over and over throughout their lifetimes. Such conversations do not make violence more palatable. And it is probable that one can't do enough to prevent future terrorist attacks…or to do away with violence in the creature's world. But one can do what one can do, and some of these educational activities are deeply grounded in theology.

For example, the creature's Christian religious experience offers a world that is inclusive not only of evil and violence, but also of joy, goodness, dynamics of gentleness, blessings that come through little kindnesses, and celebrations that also preoccupy daily agendas. Anna Quindlen (2002) wrote a piece noting that her son's birthday was September 11. Her immediate culture carried both realities: the pleasure and delight of a child growing up, and the reality and awfulness of a destructive force that brought ongoing pain to many. As pastoral care with victims of sexual abuse sought to invite them not only to be survivors but also caregivers themselves, so might we work with survivors of such events as these over time. In this sense the victims of horrific evils join those who suffer from irreversible chronic conditions or illnesses in modeling a way to live in a world of broken hearts with hearts also filled with compassion, joy, and love. One cannot simply produce or even shape that desired experience. One can, however, witness to its reality and there are plenty of survivors' stories that bear such witness. Perhaps they can be better heard if we are assured that the stories of those who lose their dignity and experience the burdens of victimization, oppression, and violence are also truly heard. That is why we begin these essays with death and catastrophe.

Among the practices of care it is also to be hoped that caregivers and receivers will be present in the extensive public discourse that accompanies these issues. But that is for a later essay.

Finally, I note that care of the creature is inclusive of the terrorist, the murderer, the abuser, the perpetrator of horrendous violence. At present the International Justice system located in The Hague is considering the horrendous crimes and evils that were perpetuated in the Balkans in the 1990s. A major perpetrator has the right to serve as his own lawyer. The primary response was not one of retaliation, but the processes of justice were set in motion to determine appropriate legal, moral, and cultural response. A terrorist recently identified himself in *The New York Times* saying that while he would not bring acts of terror to innocent persons, he would be a terrorist until his death or his madness. We are left with Volf's recognition that we may approach these issues differently from within zones of safety than within locations where the people involved have directly experienced acts of violence and evil. Pastoral care carries the challenge of addressing issues of forgiveness, certainly theologically, but also functionally, in order that new genealogies of violence will not be developed and carried throughout ongoing generations. But that topic is itself one of complex dynamics, certainly one of the many perspectives to be considered in emerging understandings of education for care!

A Major Refusal

The title of Marilyn McCord Adams's book *Horrendous Evils and the Goodness of God* (1999) has remained with me through my reflections. Let us anticipate a few of the issues that will be developed later. First, grounded in creation, finitude is not the only mark of creative processes. Creation carries more than violence and evil, whether embodied in the forces of nature (violence in the natural order) or evil (intentional acts that refuse the dignity of the creature). Thus suffering is not the only quality that God shares with the creatures; there is also joy and awe, possibility and kindness, love and pleasure. Dynamics of guilt and shame can repress these realities; as we shall see, neurosis will block the experience of joy.

What seems most important theologically is to refuse a view of creation and history that makes history and finitude themselves evil. Such a move robs the creature of the "Moreness" that is present, both within and beyond the creature's limited orbit of meaning. The oppressed also play. The survivors of Auschwitz gathered to praise God. The first birthdays of the babies born after their fathers were killed were celebrations of joy—along with the ongoing grief. This refusal needs to be combined with a view of the intrinsic presence of death, chronicity, crisis, and, yes, even violence and evil, as historical realities or tragedies within the human situation that can be received and lived through. This takes the focus off perennial grapplings with theodicies that ultimately seek to explain the ways of God and protect God: two quite arrogant activities. This is done by creating an understanding of sin that itself can be oppressive and lead to violence as the "saved" need to deal with the "sinners," sometimes by destroying them so that the utopia that God intends will come, or the paradise that was lost can be regained. Thus we come full circle to a realization that throughout history and including today humans may use violence as a way to prevent violence.

How much easier it was when pastoral care appeared to be kindly ways of connecting creature and Creator through modes of healing and sustaining, guiding and reconciling. Yet how blessed we are to care so deeply for the entirely beautiful creature that we seek to enter into the created world as given, thankfully within the perspectives of a historical faith and the reality of a historical Savior.

Finitude and Limitation

I have described the living human creature as finite, limited, and historically situated. I have also commented on pastoral care and theology as dimensions of a search to better understand the creature (the human condition), the world, and God. I have begun here intentionally, not only because such situations of limitation are predominant in the practices of pastoral care, but also because I want to speak of the creature's joy and playfulness, in the goodness of God, by not ignoring, masking, sentimentalizing, or minimizing the fragility and peril the creature faces and the encounter with brute reality that in some way marks every human pilgrimage.

I have also briefly presented and commented upon the many vocations and modes of care, and argued for recognition of the importance of a great variety of partners in the caring enterprise. Institutions other than the church participate in both direct services and the nuances of care: hospitals, facilities for special groups such as the aging or teenagers, special places for persons with mental illnesses or AIDS, Planned Parenthood, a variety of self-help groups, hospices, funeral homes, and many more. The resources, too, are finite and limited, not only financially but in terms of caregivers who offer ordinary kindnesses, frequently as important as highly specialized care. We have begun to see how caring institutions—and the many urgent needs related to finitude and limitation—require connection between the private, i.e., religious or sectarian, and the public service worlds. Legislation is important, and participation in public legislative processes involves conserving and liberating voices representing the creature's many needs for care. Situations of finitude and limitation also present a variety of needs, levels of service, etc., that require sophisticated discernments about matching needs and resources. Most also carry prophetic concerns as well.

A description of the worlds of the creature has also been attempted, connecting the kinds of worlds with the kinds of care. For example, a broken world states relational inequalities, a loathsome world makes finitude and history themselves evil, a world that finds the creature responding with shock and anxiety to its situation posits, then, a world in which the creature acts to preserve itself in inordinate concern for self. Sin becomes part of the dimension. We have tried to present a world of natural and historical/cultural forces and dynamics that is frequently inhospitable to the creatures, who perennially find themselves in fragile and perilous situations.

There can be a variety of responses to those worlds, and at various points the creature denies its own limitation, surrenders meekly in the face of adversity, or consents to its place in the created order, as creature, living out of a creaturely stance, instead of as God, the Creator. Thus the modes of care do not cure the situation of creaturehood, even as they are grounded in understandings of the creativities, possibilities, and pleasures of the creature's finite existence. For the Christian faith is one of historical embodiment, where God entered history and culture as described in the brokenness above, and thus created a world where ultimacy and immediacy traffic together. Incarnation represents both real God and real creature. This presence of grace within the same dynamics as those of physical creation brings positive energies into the world both in Jesus of Nazareth and in the abiding presence of the Spirit, which are to be claimed along with the many sufferings.

The evils of the world present new forms of challenge that appear for each generation, such as today's pluralism; violence and the recognition that all religious life carries a dark undertone; advances in science and technology, which some understand as shifting from creaturehood toward pretending to be God; and a globalization not only of economy but of radical identity differences. Let us recall that movement 1 seeks to fully recognize the creature's fragility and the horrendous evils that accompany creaturely existence, the rude and brutal awakenings and forces that deny the creature's aspirations and expectations. What then shall we say to this of joy, hope, and goodness?

We now move into movement 2, where the complexities of the creature's identity formation and community living accompany the continual need for moral focus and ethical decision making in both private and public worlds. Each of these is grounded in finitude and limitation, for we dare not move too rapidly toward a celebration of joy and goodness, lest their grounding be the thin ice that is deceptive.

On Identity and Community

The Shocks of Otherness

Love one another we must—but let no one underestimate the difficulties of the task.

How are these entirely beautiful creatures to form themselves and learn to live with one another, as well as with the otherness of their Creator and other forms of life within which they share a perilous world?

Here the essays take off in a somewhat different direction: If the first movement deals with areas usually associated with pastoral care, this set of essays deals with pastoral issues that have frequently been viewed as more specialized, such as pastoral counseling in its several forms, the practices and use of systems theory and conflict management, guides as to how to make ethical decisions, particularly in a pluralistic world, and the ways in which the Christian carries caring responsibilities into the role as public person, citizen.

If movement 1 intentionally focuses on finitude and limitation, movement 2 intentionally focuses upon the creature as a relational being. Born out of sexual relationship, the infant carries within it the history of its ancestors, deeply embedded in chromosome, gene and hormonal bindings, racial/ethnic characteristics, gender. At birth the human creature is also born into several communities, or networks of communities, which carry within them the stories/narratives of ancestors as well as perspectives on who they are to become and how they are to live. The creature's own biochemical wiring intends relationship; indeed, the human infant would not survive without relational care—required for an extended period of time. The receiving community seeks to "raise it up in the way that it should be"; frequently without self-consciousness and always without the creature's participation, for at these early formative stages it is without ego or voice, language or options. Birth itself sets in motion perennial processes of dealing with otherness, for different communities and cultures carry different stories and narratives, expectations, views of God, and self-evident truths about how people are to be raised and taught to live together. As we shall see, identity processes usually occur through learning who one is not, which then necessitates a difficult, if not life-long, process in order to later receive who one is not as sister/brother. Often religious shapings take pride in not being one of the wrongly led others, and generations of enmity are passed down as readily and unself-consciously as the accustomed cultural foods are prepared and served.

These essays are interconnected with those of the first movement, and our understanding of the history and theological groundings of pastoral care will continue to be informative and challenging. The subject of our case—the entirely beautiful creature—is both burdened and gifted by otherness, as with finitude and limitation.

Beginning with *identity,* we will consider how the human person and personality are shaped and formed, referring to—but not developing—understandings of developmentalism and personality theory, which have been the primary interpretive tools for the practices of pastoral counseling. We will consider the various goals of individuality, independence, autonomy and community, interdependence and belonging, and present some of the basic understandings of the relation of identity to otherness. For what kind of a world is the creature being formed and prepared? How are caring practices of identity formation affected by contemporary cultural issues, especially those of pluralism and violence?

In attending to issues of *community* or association, we will focus on how human creatures are to live together, not forgetting the phrase that introduces this movement: "Love one another we must, but let no one underestimate the difficulties of the task." We will remind ourselves of streams of experience and orbits of meaning—which carry cultural understandings of church, school, congregation, and family—as well as of the communities of men and women, of sexual orientation, of religious and faith groupings. The creature is presented throughout as intrinsically relational and communal, living always at the brink of blessing and edge of curse.

In the creature's struggles to live in its world, it must also be *decisional*, and we will present the creature as *moral*, raised from birth to be decisional and caring in the ways of its shapings, concerned about issues of good and bad. We will note studies of moral development, but will focus on pastoral care as guidance in making accessible the importance of ethical decision making in a pluralistic world, and the substances in which ethical issues are grounded.

And finally we will look at the caring responsibilities and resources of *public discourse*, stepping into church and cultural issues as they are affected by, and can be understood by, caring perspectives on our finite, historical, limited, relational, communal, moral, and decisional creature. Once again, as movement 1 grounded our move toward joy, celebration, play, and goodness even in the midst of the brute realities that mask them, so will movement 2 express what may seem to be the impossibility of human community. It will also claim possibilities for the creature's creative and positive contributions within the creation in which it has been so lovingly placed. Momentarily utilizing the metaphor of God as parent, I note that parents hopefully choose to bring their child into a world and place it lovingly within all the possibilities and problematics of existence, unable to prevent its woes and constrained not to abandon it.

The Living Human Creature

Issues of Identity and Formation

Novelists and therapists, fathers and mothers (and grandparents!) holding a newborn, theologians seeking to understand the nature of God, ordinary pastors seeking to preach what God expects, and everyday Christian education teachers hoping to form a Christian creature—each ponders and carries perspectives on the issues and nature of identity.

There is general agreement that the creature's identity is social. Volf states it as clearly as anyone:

The identity of a person is inescapably marked by the particularities of the social setting in which he or she is born and develops. In identifying with parental figures, peer groups, teachers, religious authorities, and community leaders, one does not identify with them simply as human beings, but also with their investment in a particular language, religion, customs, their construction of gender and racial difference, etc. (1996, 19)

Fifty years ago Meland (1953) spoke of this as the creature being born into particular "orbits of meaning" that carry the history and values of the family and local culture (or tribe). This orbit has already shaped the childcare practices that form the infant to be what is considered desirable. On a broader scale, these more local orbits are carried within a broader stream of experience, which is, for example, the history of the culture of a nation or even a part of the world. Deep within the fabric of everyday life are differences between being shaped in an Eastern/Hindu tradition rather than, say, in Western/Christian perspectives.

These shapings bind the creature into the world that surrounds it and defines its situatedness. The expectations that go with being a girl or a boy, a member of a tribal family or a member of a family of autonomous individuals, are carried here. How one is to relate to the individual, tribal, or national God is communicated through nursing practices and childcare, toilet training practices and nursery friendships, birthday parties and desirable behaviors in house of worship.

The local nature of identity formation was not as clear when I first studied pastoral care. The understandings of growth and development were generally assumed to be universal. For several decades pastors and pastoral counselors sought to shape persons through perspectives on growth that assumed that institutions and cultural expectations were oppressive. That generation seemed to focus upon issues of self, that is, self-worth, self-naming, self-actualization, self-awareness. This very Western value was related to deeply evolving understandings of the role of the individual in culture and the possibilities that a free "man" carried to cure disease, establish democratic government, "make the world safe for democracy," deliver the gospel throughout the world. Such identity shapings live on in congregations.

Shifts of expectation as to who the human being should become are not new. At issue is how they might be named for this generation with its concerns about care for the mortal, guilty, entirely beautiful creature living into the twenty-first century. After attending to some perspectives on the history of working with identity issues within pastoral care, I will suggest the need for a shift in the perspectives that state the desired outcomes of identity formation. In a world that recognizes the creature's vulnerability to death, chronicity, crisis, and even the horrors of violence, the creature may need more courage and support than is presently recognized. Values of persistence and endurance may re-emerge. In addition, the creature is vulnerable to other creatures, shaped differently within cultures threatening to one's own. Excesses of individualism have left some creatures without community, or disdaining the communities available to them. Creatures priding themselves on their openness to creatures other than themselves have difficulty understanding why they themselves are experienced as a threat, even as enemy.

Volf's *Exclusion and Embrace* (1996) is one of the perspectives, an identity that is not generally a part of conversations about identity in the field of pastoral care. He views the ways in which the issues of identity and difference are resolved as determinative of the future of the world itself. In some identity formation processes, the other may become strange or dangerous, having to be translated into one's own categories to be understood. In this translation, otherness is lost. Practices of exclusion rooted in suspicion of others bring about domination and oppression, deception and violence. The issues of pluralism and globalization, conflicts concerning developments in science and technology, and violence within religions are clearly interconnected with ordinary pastoral care. What are the valued goals of identity formation? Who is the creature to become? How are they to get along with other creatures, not only strange ones but even creatures very much like themselves? How is a world to be shared?

Volf is quite clear what is needed: "[T]he will to give ourselves to others" and welcome them, to readjust our identities to make space for them, is prior to any judgment about others, except that of identifying them in their humanity. The *will to embrace* precedes any truth about others and any construction of their justice. This will is absolutely indiscriminate and strictly immutable; it transcends the moral mapping of the social world into good and evil.

If this analysis is to be credited, shifts in the values that attend identity formation and developmental process need to be considered. For example, along with autonomy might be considered courage, and along with self-actualization, self-sacrifice. There might even be additions to existing models of sound mental health or wholeness. Some might come from the identity of those who have received chronic illness with courage and hope, experiencing joy and relationships, possible activities and blessings. Others might come from those who serve others, not out of slavery but out of compassion. There might be new attention paid to the notion of sacrifice in caring for children and the elderly with sacrifice a valued part of developmental process, at least when one covenants to raise children and care for the elderly as shared tasks. First, let us glance at pastoral care practices and theoretical understandings as pastoral care has ministered in the areas of identify formation.

Pastoral Care and Identity Formation

It may be hard to conceive, but viewing the creature as a growing and developing human organism is relatively new. When I studied with Seward Hiltner in the 1950s, his lectures at the edge of knowledge were about understanding the formation of human identify through developmental processes. From the beginning the distinction was made between growth, as simply unfolding, and development, as continual engagement of the organism with the culture around it, being shaped and reshaped by cultural influences upon the infant-child-adolescent and through to the processes of aging. This developmental view has become normative and often accepted as self-evident, without critique. But looked at with "Volf-like" eyes, two considerations leap out.

First, the processes of development include negatives, that is, who I should *not* be, whom I should *not* become. I am girl, not boy; heterosexual, not homosexual; Christian, not Jew; perhaps even fundamentalist Christian, not liberal Christian; American and not Palestinian; etc. That some such clarity is important in identity process I do not dispute. But the visions and values of religion and culture frequently leave it at that, not recognizing that the developmental expectations farther down the line expect the creature to joyfully welcome the one that he or she is not, to share a world with that one, to be hospitable to one whose tribal identity has been defined as enemy, and to embrace those who have been excluded from one's own identity processes. On a personal level, caring practices have emerged to accompany persons whose learnings about what they were not were oppressive. For example, persons of homosexual orientation, many women, have had to overcome alienating oppression and embrace a dimension of themselves.

Volf's concerns involve what kind of selves we need to be to live in harmony with these others, perhaps already defined in terms of threat or enemy. My concern is only slightly different: What kind of selves do we have to be to live in association with others, with the perspective of first do no harm, so that cities such as Sarajevo, Beirut, New York, and Jerusalem might at least find enclaves of otherness that respect one another's right to existence without the need to destroy them or force them into becoming like selves? Such work is more difficult than it appears at first sight. The Christian vision expects intimate community, perhaps even a culture of utopian hope, the reign of God, a return to Eden. What is possible may be quite different, especially in the world of finitude and limitation that we are describing and in which the human creature actually lives.

But here we are focusing on issues of identity and not community. Within those parameters a slight shift of viewpoint will demonstrate very different cultural ways of defining childhood. In North American culture there is the luxury of postponing the movement or transition from childhood into adulthood for a very long time indeed. Thus children are not expected to deal with vulnerabilities of death and violence, and we are not sure how to both raise our young to receive strangers, and to be perennially aware of strangers as potentially dangerous. Death and violence, then, come to many as a surprise, as was illustrated in the reactions to the events in Oklahoma City and lower Manhattan. While Americans know that they die, many expect that technology will conquer death—at least in *my* case! So death, viewed as an intrusion, becomes a threat to individual and national identity, formed in cultural processes that have been able to exclude death and violence, but also should have been prevented.

Our identity processes have also postponed the need to learn how to embrace the other until one's own identity is in good shape. But since conceptually that doesn't happen until after adolescence, and the expectation of generativity is kept for the older adult, children may not learn the need for courage, persistence, and self-sacrifice. Their responsibilities within their family, church, or tribe, and the reality that they do not carry an entitlement to prosperity or special fortune offered by their God, may not be made known until they experience the shocks of finitude and limitation in some devastating way.

Second, looked at through Volf's eyes, these processes of identity formation should focus more upon the kind of agent being formed, rather than upon the content that grounds the identity. In other words, he changes the focus from a concentration on social arrangements to a focus on social agents.

Instead of reflecting on the kind of society we ought to create in order to accommodate individual or communal heterogeneity, I will explore what kind of selves we need to be in order to live in harmony with others. My assumption is that selves are situated. They are female or male, Jew or Greek, rich or poor—as a rule, more than one of these things at the same time (rich Greek female), often having hybrid identities (Jew-Greek), and, sometimes, migrating from one identity to another. The questions I will be pursuing about such situated selves are: How should they think of their identity? How should they relate to the other? How should they go about making peace with the other?

Thus, Volf challenges practical theologians of pastoral care: "Theologians should concentrate less on social arrangements and more on fostering the kind of social agents capable of envisioning and creating just, truthful, and peaceful societies, and on shaping a cultural climate in which such agents will thrive" (1996, 21).

He suggests a sustained theological dialogue on social agents. What kind of agents are Christian educators seeking to fashion? What does it mean—in terms of the particularities of identity formation—for Brita Gill-Austern to seek the formation of followers of Jesus Christ who live in shalom with neighbor, self, God, and all of creation? As pastoral care has come to include concern for liturgy and ritual, the questions of identity formation shift from psychological goals to agents (disciples?) of social peace. It may well be that the capacity to embrace others is connected to issues of self-worth and self-acceptance, but it is problematic if these must be prior to a formation of identities that can live with joy this side of the promised land. Volf himself argues for the importance of resources to live within a culture of endurance, not only a culture of social hope. Often pastoral care has joined with those who expect the historical realization of the marvelous vision of the "one table" that includes all of humanity. More frequently pastoral care practitioners are well aware of the vulnerabilities, sufferings, and unfulfillment of their entirely beautiful creatures, but have not found a way to express this perennial historical reality in satisfactory theological or pastoral ways.

Some Helpful Practices

The contemporary practices of pastoral care have been founded upon respect for the living human document, and for listening to the stories of human creatures. A complex hermeneutic of narration has grounded much of pastoral counseling's practices with individuals, and both marriage and family therapy have pondered family stories and their effect upon present identity. Pastoral care recognizes the ways in which marriages bring together different cultures that must learn how to live peacefully together. Of great interest to me was a recent meeting of Interfaith Partnership of Metropolitan St. Louis, presenting a forum on "Caring Conversations in the Midst of Crisis." Note the similarity to traditional pastoral care concerns in the suggested topics offered to the participants:

How/what are you feeling?
How do we hear/listen to each other?
How do we care for each other during this difficult time?
How do we stay in relationship?

Often pastoral care's common practices of listening to histories/ stories and attending to feelings appear too ordinary to connect to major cultural issues. This is a missed opportunity both ways. Probably something that is less demanding and takes less time would be more welcomed!

Ed Friedman (1985) argues that his view of family process is both ecumenical and, in its cultural inclusiveness, universal. While this approach does not readily translate to other cultures, as I have experienced with my international students, its focus upon differentiation while at the same time being able to belong is suggestive. Certainly one of the identity issues in encountering otherness is to be able to do so without experiencing a debilitating threat, however risky. The old perspective that "one must have a self in order to lose a self" comes to mind. However, in present conversation this is too linear, too much connected to successful identity formation, instead of being a dimension of the formation processes themselves. Thus generativity is too precious to await the final developmental stage. And if care is itself a definer of humanity, then its practices are unrelated to age.

We live in a world where children do experience violence and where death no longer needs to be hidden. More and more grandparents die in hospice situations, and tragedies that affect schools are attended by processes of grief counseling. The powerful cultural issues that are shaping social and political agendas cause one to beware of one's own certainties even while living out of faithful groundings in the goodness of God. The issues and their complexity—while not a new dynamic within human history—nevertheless are experienced newly by this generation. Instead of expecting answers, formation processes might focus more upon perspectives. Even as scripture places creatures as living in between creation and its fulfillment, promise (or vision) and everyday existence, a goal of identity formation might be the capacity to learn different ways in different settings without a loss of authenticity or integrity. A creature that does not need certainty may be better prepared for living in a perilous world with knowledge of its own mortality than one that seeks instant answers and *the* truths of existence. Identity formation, then, becomes more of a nuanced process than a linear progression. It is fraught with dangers, and wrought out rather than given. Often composed of fragments, it is able—even in its fragmentation—to recognize that it is not God. Volf has his own point of view about this:

> The thesis about the correspondence between divine and human action rightly underlines that the fundamental theological question in relation to violence is the question about God: "What is God like?"—the God who "loves enemies and is the original peace maker" (Yoder) or the God of vengeance, out to punish the insubordinate? The thesis has, however, one small but fatal flaw: humans are not God. There is a duty prior to the duty of imitating God, and that is the duty of *not wanting to be God*, of letting God be God and humans be humans. (1996, 301)

There is a final comment about the dynamics of pastoral care practices. Pastors and laity, counselors and chaplains have noticed that negation and hatred are carried deeply within identity processes. The theological and cultural shaping against homosexuality, for example, has been carried generation to generation until it becomes almost impossible in some settings to discuss it. More benign attitudes exist in relation to other issues. Those raised in a "yellow dog democrat" family carry a hostility toward Republicans that cuts off dialogue. It has taken more than half a century for those identified with baptism as immersion to receive those who sprinkle, and identities are variously framed by beliefs and doctrines. Pruyser reminds us that our beliefs become a part of our identities, and we are passionate about them. Even as we love or identify with our beliefs, we may hate or deny alternative beliefs, and in some situations be prepared to die or kill for them. It has recently been recognized that different forms of worship are preferred by persons of different identity formations, and that fixity exerts as much power as the dynamics of change. This becomes part of the givenness of the creature as a dimension of creation itself, for the creature, as we have seen, is finite, limited, and historical. The creature is also intrinsically relational, unable to live or exist without the care, touch, companionship of other creatures. Yet this states a further problematic and limitation, for the creature has to learn to live with and receive others, even those who at first appear to be a threat to its own identity.

Some Possibility for the Identities of Intrinsically Relational Creatures

For an intrinsically relational being, even ordinary kindnesses affirm one's identity. The removal of this category of relationships from pastoral care has minimized our awareness of how important ordinary graciousness, everyday recognitions, and little kindnesses are for hospitable culture. This may be one of the graces of the small church and neighborhood, deeply missed in expressing values such as "it takes a neighborhood to raise a child." Yet even now, wherever we are, awareness and appreciation of the creature and its relational needs can guide our conduct at hospital admissions desks, in the elevator, meeting with a teacher when both teacher and parent are exhausted, and remembering that your secretary is entirely beautiful!

A common complaint of pastors is their lack of friends. Restricted by their office and by the aura of holiness that surrounds them, pastors frequently hunger after friends to go fishing with, to go to flea markets with, to watch television with, or to share an interest in collecting stamps or reading murder mysteries. Marriages, families, and denominational resources may not be able to meet these quite ordinary human needs Pastors will often hope for something not heavy, professional, or arranged—more like the spontaneity that can be present in friendship and everyday recognitions.

There is a danger in presenting only utopian perspectives for meaningful relationships. Whether liberal or conservative, the vision is frequently mistaken for an achievable historical possibility, and that which is given that does not live up to the vision can be overlooked or disdained. Further, its absence can lead to cynicism and despair, anxiety and even nihilism, as unfulfilled expectations turn into entitlement denied. Most relationships are not those of therapeutic intimacy or pastoral intentionality, and those should not be a norm.

It is important for identity to be aware of and find some meaning in the tribe into which one has been born. With the exception, of course, of abuse, formation processes which focus on self-actualization can separate the creature from its own roots, which remain a longing even when being intellectually rejected. When parents are always to blame for one's failings or feelings, one loses the connection that is there and the history that it carries. If one's identity has to be self-made, the denial of its relational creation can bring feelings of abandonment rather than those of freedom. It helps to take a systems view, that is, to be able to see through the eyes of more than oneself, to experience the world, say, as one's grandmother might, or as a sibling did—and does. This is certainly practice for being able to receive the many other strangers who inhabit our many worlds.

A creature may come to recognize the hatreds and negativities that have been carried in the history of one's family or tribe. Perhaps each of us has to break away from such histories in order to embrace the many others who share the world with us—or, viewing things through others' eyes, it is we who share a world with them! Perhaps some of us can learn to live in between generations, that is, maintaining an identity that can enter or lean into the worlds of the generations before and after us—as well as the generations being lived out by those whom we have been raised to hate or disdain. In such ordinary practices lie practicing for the possibility of "nonviolent embrace without end" which is Volf's own vision—or utopia.

In such ordinary concerns, one may find new identity models. The three that I will suggest are, unfortunately, not highly valued at present. The first is the identity model of the chronically ill person who receives her bodily condition and lives on with joy and possibility, much as Christopher Reeve did. The second are the many aides who serve with kindness in nursing homes, despite their minimal wages and often invisible status in regards to the families of those whom they faithfully clean and comfort, feed and converse with. And the third model, which will be described in the next essay, are those participants in ecumenical and interfaith dialogues who have invested in enough time to get to know others, and in enough risk to stay together without prematurely leaving one another for intransigent or apparently non-negotiable differences.

This relationality of existence (as theologians would have it) also states a perspective on care that contains very clear values. For a relational creature, abandonment is the worst evil. This is the pain of those with physical disfigurements or mental incapacities, that they do not receive touch or companionship. This is the worst fear of the aging or dying: that they will be abandoned or die alone. This is what a culture in distress will do that most announces its failings: the abandonment of its children, whether to starvation or terror, orphanages or street wanderings, or the more sophisticated abandonment of children in a materialistic society that has little time or commitment to their everyday emotional needs.

In any event, the primary thrust of identity formation can no longer be the calling forth of independent and/or autonomous selves. It is rather to form creatures who can live peacefully in a violent world, able to consent to finitude and limitation while continuing to be persistent in the pursuit of justice...

A Word on Particularity

But doesn't the above dialogue remove from pastoral care its first priority, the particularity of the creatures, their non-interchangeable nature, and their idiosyncratic needs? Not at all, for we begin and we end there: Each creature is unique *and* connected, autonomous *and* belonging, individual *and* yet shaped by history and tribes that carry their own uniquenesses. These processes of care, however, are only now being clearly connected to the major theological and cultural issues that shape both academic and ecclesial worlds, and which must frame the care and devotion of ordained and lay caregivers and receivers. For it is as particular creatures that we struggle to learn to share our peril in community, making difficult decisions and daring to speak in public discourse about controversial issues.

ESSAY 6

Community, Association, and Tolerance

IS HUMAN COMMUNITY POSSIBLE?

Why can't we all just get along together? Whether in biological family or congregation, denomination or global community, a sense of surprise seems to attend rising divorce rates, congregational conflict, divided denominations, and public discourse about just war. The expectation of living within a loving fellowship of the like minded has been shattered. Pastoral care practices rightly focus on dynamics of pain and suffering, lack of self-worth and failures in communication that attend many community crises. But the discipline has much more to contribute to creatures living in the many worlds of pluralism and violence, changing contexts of decision-making and feelings that things will never be the same again. The creature is not only a living human document, but it lives collegially within a living human web.

We will take a look at the way in which various issues of community affect the everyday existence of our entirely beautiful creature, with beginning reflections on elementalism, exclusiveness, ecumenism, and embrace.

Elementalism

Auden's phrase "we must love one another or die" states an even deeper truth. We must live in community or die. As we have seen, the infant will die without the community's care, not only biologically

82

but emotionally. This recognition is deeply grounded within us: Throughout our lives we hold to grown-up fantasies of the perfect familiar embrace. Often our expectations for our biological, congregational and even nation-state families reflect this: What can this community do for me? Pastoral care practices have been complicit in enhancing this state of entitlement for the self, both by critiquing the various unfairnesses of its environment and by promising a freer self (or ego) that can negotiate its world on its own terms.

The church contributes by spending more time singing its visions than negotiating its conflicts. It spends little time teaching that learning how to live with otherness in a world without entitlement is one of the central tasks of becoming human and in facing into the world of the twenty-first century. How can the church help persons come to terms with their creaturely stance in a world of peril and vulnerability? And how can it connect its precariousness to a God of promise and hope? For many have mistaken our visions for what can be expected as real within everyday historical reality where we will die, experience bodily conditions that do not get better, and be shocked by crisis and violence. To shape identities that can incorporate this and live faithfully within various communal contexts is an urgent pastoral task.

The negative data of pastoral experiences are often kept secret. The living human drama is a struggle with others in families and congregations. They carry deep memories of hurts and suspiciousness. Within each community are harsh stories of life's fragilities and family communities that are not able to live together. Denominations are stories of brokenness and splits; interim pastors are trained to cope with intra-congregational dynamics of power struggles and relational disappointments.

Pastoral care perspectives accompany the pilgrimage of the creature through its life cycle. Its relational needs are recognized as a dimension of its creation, and pastoral care helps it deal with its disappointing or devastating community experiences. What pastoral care has not done well is to participate in the shaping of communities that can attend to the human's elemental needs for belonging in trustworthy communities of care where it can be nurtured toward wholeness and learn how to live with others. The contemporary focus has been on strengthening an autonomous self, an aware ego, a liberated person who will then attend to issues of community. These processes are integral within the discipline; at issue is the beginning point and the acknowledged goal, for coming to terms with the reality of sharing worlds with threatening others cannot await maturity. In the twenty-first century this is an urgent task!

Exclusion

There is no question but that the communities that form the individual can be toxic. We learn of programs to form suicide bombers that focus on the glories of death and the importance of sacrifice toward a greater good. We recall the unquestioned cultural shaping of women to be helpmates to men and of minorities to know their place in relation to a dominant group. Persons who are homosexual have been defined as failures in normal developmental processes. If many contemporary cultural critics are accurate, many communities are founded on the dynamics of exclusion and validated by reference to their deities.

Ordinary congregations deserve care as they work on such issues in their particular places. For these are not primarily issues of individual development. The members of the Tennessee church we've been looking at understand themselves to be "a caring community of equality and grace." Surely most congregations could affirm this, as they sing, "In Christ there is no East or West, in him no south or north, but one community of love throughout the whole wide earth."

Yet for this particular church to live out its own story proved to be difficult and divisive. To embody its value of inclusion carried a high cost: persons, and their money and years of friendship, left the church. Two staff members took cuts in pay. There were no guarantees that making this risky move toward justice would help the church grow or expand its ministry. Everyone involved was forced into dialogue about difficult issues and reflection on what had been abstract theological concepts. The congregation had to ponder its own identity, as a voluntary organization and in relation to its history, denominational involvements, and place within the communities of faith in its geographic location. Did it want to become known as a gay church? And in the midst of this, the finite creatures experienced ordinary death and limitation of illness, Sunday school lessons that discussed the prodigal son through the eyes of Henri Nouwen, reflections on the events of September 11, and quite ordinary planning for baptisms and weddings. Life went on—as it did after the crisis and the living out of its decision.

Within this congregational community, participants learned how hard it is to accept the other, and how deeply the threat of the other has been presented in history. They learned that the family stories of ordinary Christians carried knowledge that they had not felt free to share, how economics is always involved in acts of justice, and how care and justice perspectives are inevitably entangled. They discovered that they were inexperienced in ethical deliberation, although they wanted to act morally and do that which was right or good.

Slowly and over time many such communities have struggled to connect who they are to what it means to be an inclusive caring community. In many congregations, their first experience with ethnic difference has come through international adoptions. Practices of care have come to accompany the recognition that adoptive families need recognition, and care practitioners have offered not only counseling but ritual recognition. Congregations that have included persons with mental illness or developmental disability have found themselves enriched and newly challenged—both in unanticipated ways. Practices of exclusion that had been taken for granted are revealed as contrary to the visions sung and presented in scripture. A pastoral care that carries concern for community formation will focus some of its resources on nurturing and educating toward that end, and being available to listen to the voices of fear and discontent that experience threat to their safe communities of like selves.

While we will later talk about pastoral care's particular resources in the area of community, as in systems theory, marriage counseling, and so on, here we will note the possibility for pastoral care to incorporate the perspectives of the ecumenical and interfaith movements. Here is the one place in culture where diversity is lived and not only preached as God's good gift. Here strangers are viewed as friends and that which appears as threat is made real and worked with through dialogue and shared worship. And as my church in Tennessee had to invest time and painful dialogue to embody its mission statement, so do any caring practices that carry the hope of transformation require a similar investment.

Ecumenism

Since the creature is born and shaped in community, the literatures of care need to attend positively to the shapings of religious community. For some decades, certain understandings taught within pastoral care suggested looking for the demonic within such shapings, that is, where the person's God had become oppressor, or the person carried inordinate feelings of guilt and shame that had come from misperceptions, or misteachings, about who the creature was in relation to God. Pastors and counselors listened for psychological instead of theological themes in the stories of their parishioners and clients, and educational programs for pastors and laity focused on psychological rather than theological awareness.

But for a hundred years, now, persons committed to inclusive community have engaged in dialogue and sought after ways that different faith groups can with integrity participate in processes that lead toward the understanding that the one God has fashioned a creation marked by wondrous complexity and a single human family marked by natural diversities (e.g., of race and sex). It is precisely our basic commonality, as bearers of God's image, that ought to make it possible for us to perceive the manifold particularity of human life as gift rather than threat.

This movement recognizes that creatures turn to their communities for support in attaining right identity, that is, identity that brings favor with their God. Radical differences have existed as to what is right in these perspectives, having to do with life cycle issues such as baptism and death practices, marriage and gender roles. Issues of governance have divided those who understand the role of bishops as intrinsic in creation and those who "know" that God prefers local church polity. Recognizing the elementalism of creatures in the world, as well as their tendencies toward exclusion, the ecumenical movement has sought to bring together—or at least engage in dialogue—creatures who have found a variety of ways to live in a perilous creation. By committing themselves to remain together over time out of a common affirmation of One God, they have moved toward quite astonishing shared perspectives on how it is possible for creatures to live together, through their differences, in a world of continual peril and threat. With the ecumenical virtues of persistence and courage, and of endurance and faith groundings, a model of working toward caring has been developed that has not yet become an intrinsic dimension of pastoral care.

Meland's categories are helpful here, as we seek after caring ways in which human community becomes possible in a world of exclusion. Shaped by radically different orbits of meaning, the creature must intentionally engage in a process of meeting those whom it has been carefully taught it is *not*: (homosexuals, Muslims, fundamentalists, Republicans). Of course those others must also experience the same revisions, for one of the hidden issues in identity formation is the need to eventually recognize oneself as enemy in the perspective of these others. That is, it is not only that I must find processes to receive the other; I must also realize that to many others *I* am stranger, enemy, threat, evil one. It is only slowly and over time that such perceptions can change, for, in relation to some understandings of women and religious faith, *I am* enemy, however I may choose not to commit acts of terrorism on my behalf. Far too much of pastoral care's perspectives have only gone one way—to shape the creature to be more like that which is familiar to me and mine, rather than attending to processes by which I might become less a threat to them.

One of the groundings for this perspective is to claim an ethic of mutuality and equal regard. Within such an ethic care giver and care receiver are one, as we have already noted. Anyone willing can come to table and be heard. The shaping of community is a shared practice and even boundaries are openly drawn.

One of the ironies of the pastoral care movement has been that the most ecumenical and interfaith practices have been developed by chaplains who frequently occupy a marginal relationship with the guild's professional system. In military settings, chaplains are obligated to work together in interfaith structures and practices. Here may be the only place where the various fundamentalisms and liberalisms within each religious faith cooperate, plan programs together, work out shared responsibilities collegially, and intend to meet their own faith's needs while being respectful of the many others.

Of course this does not work perfectly, but it is real and valued by secular law. Yet military chaplains are seldom included within the denominations and faith groups that endorse them, and almost never are they sought out to serve on ecumenical and interfaith commissions—or to participate in conversations seeking to redefine pastoral care. Even within the hospital system local pastors and hospital chaplains move in separate worlds, although the chaplains, too, are required to work respectful of the many faiths that come to hospital settings. Here live conversations ponder the meaning and desirable rituals for stillbirths, organ transplants, turning off life support systems, and being present with the many cultural styles by which families receive the reality of death. I have argued elsewhere that the hospital may be viewed as today's cathedral, a center where secularism and sectarianism meet in the service of creatures experiencing the various shocks of finitude and limitation that invariably attend their existence and inevitably show up in medical settings. Here, too, is a fertile ground for ecumenical and interfaith dialogue, for all experience the vulnerabilities of death and seek to be informed participants out of scientific and theological/faith perspectives.

While there is some overlap, the teachers of pastoral care are not inclusive of chaplains, nor do the organizations of specialized pastoral counselors normatively include chaplains and interfaith participants. Yet if we speak of a world where dealing with the relations between identity and otherness are crucial to survival, the absence of ordinary pastoral care practitioners, that is, local pastors and laypersons, is inconceivable. Seminary courses in pastoral care that are taught by professors and chaplains, professors and informed ecumenical and/ or interfaith spokespersons, professors and laity active in practices of care, are a beginning in a dialogue so crucial for the discipline of pastoral care.

Embrace

In seeking to meet the elemental needs of the creature, as well as to shape the creature toward desired ends, various communities seek to understand their differing roles. This focuses the family debate within the United States, as some theorists deplore the slippery slope into immorality and disdain of the Christian family, and others celebrate the variety of family forms that are emerging. The emerging issues appear to be those of the formation of persons/creatures who can embrace rather than exclude otherness. This is why Volf seeks to shift the argument from preferable social arrangements, that is, a particular family form, toward agents who can participate in the calling forth of communities of inclusion and care, peaceful communities of justice and diverse stories. But the focus is upon the processes of making some semblance of this possible within historical existence, rather than cynicism about the possibility, nihilism that it doesn't matter anyway, or despair that one has already tried and failed, so why try again.

The capacity for such embrace can live within the results of successful developmental processes or within the moral context of a people out of which it shapes its young. Generally following developmental perspectives, the emergence of the generative self must await decades of experience and, probably, become vital just when the life energies are diminishing, i.e., it is the last stage. As developmental processes seek to eke out a self in the midst of social and cultural complexities, its fragility may be more celebrated than its strengths. Thus the emerging child needs continual care, ever available resources, its own set of drugs and therapies, devoted attention when crisis hits, and early experiences valuing disdain toward those with differing points of view in order to establish its own identity. The harshness of this is intended; these practices of care do not seem to have produced selves vulnerable enough to receive others, egos strong enough to participate in the slow processes of change over time, or individuals truly prepared to receive those radically unlike themselves. This shows up not only in conversations about homosexuality, but in political dialogue where "the Bushes" become subjects of theological scorn. Perhaps it is that theorists such as Volf, coming out of a ravaged countryside where refusals of otherness led to horrendous devastation, have seen the results of exclusion and the absolute necessity for the formation of agents of embrace. Perhaps pastoral care's implicit moral context of individual autonomy and the self's liberation from oppression needs to shift, however slightly, to a context that values the capacity to receive otherness up front, so to speak, rather than as the result of a lengthy one-on-one therapeutic process.

To pursue this line of thought demands an appreciation of cultural forms and the importance of healthy social institutions in forming and meeting the needs of the creature. A negative view of culture is unhelpful; to view it only as created by and grounded in violence leaves the creature without resource—except for a particular theological understanding of the cross.

Within this perspective, cultural institutions become suspect, whether those of church or education, government or family. History and culture have become evil. Only death lies outside the Garden.

But the practices of pastoral care occur within institutions and cultures, and value their resources even within understanding of their own needs for transformation. The theological perspectives of Bernard Meland are again helpful. The faith and its resources are carried and witnessed to through three vortices: the individual, the *cultus* or church, and the culture itself. Not only violence but the resources of the Spirit and the energies of new being are carried in culture. And culture itself is a positive resource of sensitivity and meaning, vitality and creativity. A disdain of culture is similar to the dynamic that cannot find joy or goodness if suffering is also present, or cannot value a local church if it does not match a particular set of New Testament expectations.

Community, Association, and Tolerance

Perhaps, however, the expectations placed upon community are too high. Meland reminds us that even though we must love one another, we must never underestimate the difficulties of the task. These difficulties are witnessed to in the many community places where diversity remains threat rather than promise, where persons go away from one another as often as they seek embrace (marriage, divorce, and family life), and where local churches and denominations seem not to be able to find any common center (or plumb line or principle, or hope, etc.) upon which to stand. This situation is, of course, but another consequent dimension of the creature's creation as finite, limited, historical, and situated. Adding to this, its creation as relational and communal compounds the complexities! In the midst of this, to insist upon a community form of inclusion and intimacy, shared values and perspectives on identity, common celebrations and the particularities of shared longings, may be too much to expect.

As Martin Marty has focused on issues of the relation between the fundamentalisms and secular community, he has suggested that at least in some places, in some historical times, at some moments, the coexistence of separate communities in respectful *association* may be a possibility. In the past, cities such as Beirut, Sarajevo, New York City, and even Jerusalem have found enclaves of ethnic, racial, or religious communities living together in tolerance if not mutual respect. Some would argue that it is only when one tribe insists that its identity is normative for all, and that its God has instructed it to make that real in history, that chaos and terror emerge.

At the same time as dynamics of exclusion and intolerance have been shaping the world, there have been dynamics that inhibited the speaking of more tolerant voices. The first is the dynamic of a liberation movement that needs to respond to (or create) an enemy in relation to which its own identity can be achieved and solidified. But once the liberated person or group achieves even some modicum of its task, a new set of enemies has been developed and new waves of terrorism can erupt. South Africa appears to have avoided such catastrophe as it has moved from apartheid toward the creation of new national government and neighborhoods that find amazing cooperation among races. Zimbabwe, on the other hand, witnesses to Rosemary Reuther's classic alert to the dynamics of the oppressed becoming the oppressor. Pastoral care practices in such situations can help keep alive the perspectives that have allowed liberated women to work in partnership with men. The participation of predominantly African American denominations within ecumenical movements seeks new structures that represent values of mutuality and equal regard. Thus pastoral counselors with victims of oppression seek not to secure their survivor status through dynamics of hatred. As new freedoms are achieved, perspectives of care would value forgiveness over retaliation, but with neither being simply defined. Thus, ordinary care is connected deeply with the issues of the twenty-first century.

This dynamic is crucial in noting how hatred is carried through the stories of people and communities over the centuries. History becomes not that which happened to our ancestors centuries ago, but what is presently unfolding before our eyes, and fresh blood enacting history feeds some participants in the many communities struggling for power in the Middle East. Pastoral care perspectives, when present, though they seldom are in such situations, can serve as a moral context seeking to stem tides of violence, to cut off generational hatreds, even to risk reconciliation and forgiveness. The pastoral care historic mode of reconciliation may need re-valuation, not only in situations of marriage and divorce, but within conflicted groups within congregations, such as, say, reconciliation between those who stayed and those who left following the hiring of a pastor at my church in Tennessee. And the reconciliation processes must be viewed as two-way rather than simply me reconciled to you, for we speak of entire communities.

The second dynamic has been that of political correctness, making it easy to let go the particularity that has marked pastoral care throughout the centuries. Within the circles where I move, it is generally not "p. c." to seek to understand persons suffering from homophobia, to converse about Bush's policies without having it made clear that he is to be disdained, to care about students who not only come to seminary with the "wrong" points of view but who leave without adopting ours, or to grasp that the diversities that we value include those of persons who do not ordain women or persons who are homosexual or persons who understand that they are called to military chaplaincy. The urge toward political correctness that infects the liberal community has also led to a decrease in the positive value of tolerance. Toleration has come to mean letting justice issues go, and that has diminished the value of tolerance, which alone can allow for the coexistence of communities and cultures that will not collapse into having the same values. Martin Marty's historic work on the place of varied associations in public life may be immensely helpful to persons within pastoral care who seek to help persons, groups, and little communities toward coexistence. Some care practitioners have experience in this as they have helped divorcing parents to remain in healthy association on behalf of their children. Civility becomes a value, in private and public life. Pastoral care may find an interest in manners!

The third dynamic is the loss of any positive value to self-sacrifice. As feminism rightly shifted the understanding of self-sacrifice away from being a permanent feminine role, the move was also incisive in affecting any conversation about the nature of sacrifice itself. We are unprepared for suicide bombers, prepared to sacrifice their lives in the name of their ancestors and for the hope of the future. Coupled with centuries of sacrifice understood to be the role of wife and mother, this negative image did not invite new conversation. Hymns about the blood of Christ disappeared from hymnals, and it was the blood of menstruation rather than that of sacrifice that was celebrated.

Yet if the elemental needs of children are to be met, their parents must sacrifice something of their autonomy (and even possessions!) for a healthy family life to be possible. While the Don Browning family project has been clear from the beginning about the expectation that this sacrifice is for both parents, not just the mother, his statements of the importance of equality and equal regard have not quieted the many voices that distrust any mention of sacrifice. Family therapists have generally not spoken of sacrifice, but have noted the needs for self-differentiation so that various members of a family can both be separate and belong. This sacrifice of the perceived unity of a family allows many families to survive. Marriage and couple counselors are well aware of the need for negotiation and compromise—both forms of sacrifice—within couple partnerships. Probably the best emergent model is that of the ecumenical movement, in which participants have been able to put their own values on hold long enough to listen to one another, and have found that such processes enrich rather than demand negation for groups to worship and plan together.

For a variety of expectations within postmodernity, it is not only politically incorrect but theologically subversive for Christians to remind themselves of the importance of blood sacrifice in their historic understandings of faithfulness. Perhaps what is at stake in any contemporary understandings of sacrifice is a new beginning. First, ordinary people make daily sacrifices of their own desires and needs, and do so freely, in order for marriages and families to flourish—or at least survive. Second, sacrifice may mean only the letting go of a false perception that has been so highly valued that it has defined identity. For example, I—those like me, those who understand God like I do—hold the truth. This perception might be laid on the altar as a sacrifice before the God who William James (2004) always insists is "Moreness." I may sacrifice some of my ideals and visions of human community in order to allow, to experience tolerance for, living in proximity to human associations that do not embody my values, but with whom I share a world. One of my dear friends, quite to her surprise, now shares a world with grandchildren who are being raised as the most orthodox of Hasidic Jews. They remain her grandchildren, but may never value her ordination. As we move more deeply into finding ways in which we can stand one another rather than kill one another, new conversations about sacrifice might be helpful. To be able to let go in order that something else (perhaps that which is possible!) can become may become a newly valued goal of the creature's formation!

This sacrifice must not be that of the scapegoat who carries responsibility for evil and violence in the thought of some contemporary theorists. It may be more like the mutual sacrifice of parents and grandparents to care for their children, or that of spouses or children with fragile mates or parents who find courage to "hang in there." Acts of sacrifice may allow a person with Alzheimer's (or developmental disability or deteriorating chronic illness) to remain within the family and community context.

God's sacrifice in sharing the perils of the creature's existence might speak in new ways to creatures perennially living out their finite, limited, historic, relational, and communal creation!

Issues of Community and the Practices of Pastoral Care

Generally, the farther away we are from the primary shocks of finitude, that is, death, dying, illness, crises, reactions to violence, etc., the fewer pastoral practices there are. Thus as we move from issues of community into essays on ethics and public discourse, joy and the goodness of God, we are almost without established professional resource. It has only been recently that the practices have extended into concern for community/congregational life. Yet there are resources of perspective.

For many, the family systems approach has definitively affected pastoral care's ways of seeing. While grounded in the 1950s and associated with the lectures I heard from Seward Hiltner on developmentalism and the systems thinking of Kurt Lewin and emerging gestalt thought, the work of Ed Friedman and others has affected the ways in which pastoral care specialists view family dynamics and the ways in which some clergy view their own way of functioning within the systems of the congregation. This way of thinking is grounded in intersecting family communities, that is, the family of the rabbi or pastor, the families within church or synagogue, and the religious institution as itself family. This approach can help us view congregations themselves as in need of care. The Tennessee congregation, for example, needed healing, and much occurred through dialogue and the rituals and liturgies of worship together. In other settings, where there has been abuse by a pastor, the congregational organism is affected. While pastoral care first rightly addressed itself to the victim, with some attention to victimizer, it also recognized the effect this has upon the congregational system in which it has occurred. As I have reflected recently on the incidents of priestly abuse, I have hoped for the presence of pastoral care within those congregations most directly affected, as well as those whose identities were threatened by the apparent pervasiveness of the abuse and certainly the pervasiveness of the publicity.

More recently, connections have been made between the care that ritual can offer and the practices of pastoral care. Certainly the shapings of a people's identity are more solidly grounded here than in psychological services. These literatures have taken care to include the various shocks of finitude within them, urging ritual practitioners not to offer a phony or romantic world of resolved conflicts and embodied visions, but rather a real world of disappointed expectations and community crisis. Ritual practice must be honest. At Easter time an occasional column in *The New York Times* contrasted the Passover literature for children with the Easter books available in bookstores (albeit secular stores). Christian children, their faith grounded in resurrection, were regaled with stories of bunnies and Easter eggs, little ducks finding spring coming, and children lunging for goodies on the church's back lot, whereas the Passover texts included the stories of murdered infants and the fear, terror, and peril within the family homes as they awaited their fate. Yom Kippur becomes a time for reflection on life's unpredictability and human frailty. When do Christian children reflect on that?

The literature of preparation for marriage has come to include recognition of the joining not only of two individuals but of two cultures. Pastors are encouraged to raise these issues along with those of sexual relations and communication., for a new family is being created, with each participant carrying deeply within expectations and perspectives about a right family life that the other may not hold.

A positive development is the growing rapprochement between Christian education and pastoral care as sister disciplines. Much care arises out of the educational community and its numerous volunteers, and, on the other hand, pastoral care is coming to recognize that one of its modes is that of education. Without any expectation that education is sufficient to solve problems or that ignorance and its correction will lead to right thinking and action, there are a variety of ways in which creativity and imagination can bring to the struggling creature a greater awareness of the perils and textures, depths and resiliencies, history and expectations of the givenness of its creation. Forums on preparation for death, ways to respond to crisis, theological understandings of exclusion and embrace, and so on, offer a style of care for the creature and its place in creation that will not be offered within more traditional care and counseling perspectives. An unexpected byproduct might be an appreciative awareness of the "bigness" of creation, the "moreness" of the Creator, the gratitude that the creature might experience for life itself.

The power to shape and form us that our various communities have often makes it feel as if our values are bred in the bone. Our passions for love and hatred are not only real but express truth. Often bolstered by various scriptures and authority figures, most creatures have not been invited toward deep awareness of their plight and critical thinking about it.

Along with the duty to acknowledge that one is not God goes the obligation to recognize that there are other truths in the world than my own. In the midst of an experience of personal or tribal tragedy it is difficult to perceive that life is going on elsewhere—usually unaware of my/our devastation. When I am with my own kind, it is hard to realize how others may feel about me—or us—and that they may be going through similar processes of learning how to receive strangers and relate to otherness—and the stranger and the other may be me! Or, unlike myself, they may be learning that their way is the right and the only way, and to do otherwise is to blaspheme God. Old histories carried deeply within family and cultural identity may at any point erupt in violence that affects my everyday world, even though I am not directly involved in their realities.

As we move into contemplating joy and the goodness of God we will return to these reflections. Yet I want to end this essay with some positive recognitions.

First, it was not that many generations ago that French and German hated each other and that the ethnic identities in Europe were engaged in hundred–year wars! Forgetting history, we view present rivalries (Palestinian and Jew) as horrific and unending. Yet placed in perspective it was also not that long ago that the Blue and the Grey thought it would be impossible for a nation split by war, economics, and slavery ever to be reunited. This does not assuage pain, but it may keep alive hope, and express the reality that the creature is, indeed, an historical being. It may do this even carrying the realization that some of the old themes seem to live on perpetually—one dimension of continuing peril.

Second, the world does go on without me—and even continues when my era is being reshaped by my great-grandchildren. History forms and reforms over time; our present conceptualizations of it produce, at best, margins of intelligibility about the fullness of the record of creatures interacting with other creatures and their natural and historical environments since their creation. It should not surprise us that the "Irish problem" continues, or that entire generations may have come down on the wrong side of history. Take the origin and processes of the civil rights movement, for example.

Third, William James suggested that it is well for creatures to recognize their "ontic dependence" since they have no choice in the matter anyway! We live within a framework of givenness, even as we anticipate an ongoing movement into unknown futures. With that sense of freedom (for a recognition of limitation brings with it a type of freedom), we might practice little kindnesses in our own places, trusting their connections to the apparently larger issues that appear so threatening.

Ethical Discernments about Care

THE CREATURE AS MORAL AND DECISIONAL

Bernard Meland (1953) says that one dimension of a creaturely stance is moral earnestness, commitment to discovering what is right and good and finding within its ethical life both joy and freedom.

This positive view may not reflect some of the creature's recent challenges in having to struggle to live amidst competing perspectives and understandings of the good. The ordinary people at my church discovered this as they sought to discern the will of God to guide their hiring practices. They listened to competing scriptural interpretations, and were challenged to act justly in providing a place for one who had not been able to find any other place, even though that meant the loss of friends and fellow Christians.

In its earlier history the congregation had made ethical decisions about having open membership to persons of other races. It had publicly received persons with Down's syndrome and not hidden them from view. Some members had struggled with issues surrounding pregnancies of single persons; the congregation felt it had made some peace with gay and lesbian members who were participants but did not speak of their sexual orientation. The congregation had been gathering experience in recognizing that ethical deliberations are wrestled with and wrought out in a congregation with varying points of view. The members could not turn to one moral authority or to some established truth emerging from scientific and medical perspectives.

They were moral creatures, entrusted with the responsibilities of ethic decision making in the embodiment of their faith…in the practical, ordinary, everyday living of their lives.

Ethical decision making in the congregation is not a simple matter of adopting and applying metaphysical, philosophical, or theological principles. It is more about how to attend to the rough and ordinary finitudes of everyday life. When hospitals turned from philosophical ethics to clinical ethics, they recognized that they served a pluralistic public, and that ethical decision making had to attend to the particulars of each situation or case, and be inclusive of diverse points of view. This move toward the public arena must be a dimension of our reflections upon ethical discernments about care, although it will await focus in the next essay. Here we will attend to what goes on in congregations concerning discernments about the many practices of care.

These may be matters of guidance between pastor and parishioner or, more commonly, committees where the members decide the ethical framework to inform their teachings on sexuality to their children and youth. Or it may be an adult class reflecting on ethical issues at the end of life, including not only the requirements for direction about end of life procedures, but broader issues about access to care and the use of available resources. As we think backward to the earlier essays, we can state that every problem in pastoral care contains a moral dimension. And as we move into the next essay, we will notice that such problems are carried over into the public arena, where the pastor's role as public person and the members' various roles as citizens who practice Christianity are vital. Even as the Tennessee congregation was struggling with the ethics involved in hiring its associate pastor, the senior pastor was publicly active in opposing the death penalty, and a council member was running for public office. It is probable that they are now discussing the ethics of just war and first strike. These are all issues of care.

Congregation as Center of Moral Discourse

Deeply rooted in rabbinic and pastoral practices is the expectation that the people of God, the congregation, need moral leadership in understanding the ways that they are to live in their precarious world and relate to one another. The historic modes of guiding and reconciliation have been prominent throughout history, taking different forms in different periods. During the middle years of the twentieth century a form of guidance emerged that placed the responsibility for right actions upon individuals. This educative guidance, practiced in various psychotherapies, sought to free or liberate the self from oppressive community moral codes. In many liberal Protestant churches a deep suspicion of moralisms developed as injunctions against dancing, smoking and drinking, divorce and remarriage, prescribed gender roles and sexual behaviors (including contraception) that appeared to bind and constrict the creature, rather than to free and liberate its possibilities.

When, thanks in large part to the work of Don Browning, it became clear that the "neutral" psychotherapies were themselves value laden and that theologies carried expectations about how creatures were to relate to their God and to each other, a renewed interest in the moral dimensions of human existence came into play. Theories of moral development were laid alongside other developmental theories. It became clear that the theologies of the liberal church were themselves heavy on moral expectation: to resist racism; to receive strangers; to be an inclusive community with those who had divorced or sought abortions; to be against war, capital punishment, and for the environment.

This is a hasty brush stroke of a highly complicated picture. Frequently individuals experienced the shock of moral perplexity much as creatures experienced the shock of finitude and limitation! That is, they were unprepared for discernment about choices in the midst of options. Congregations, too, frequently found themselves without resources in conversations about homosexuality where competing ethical perspectives could shatter community calm and trust. They lacked resources to do practical moral thinking, and the therapeutic disciplines could not fill the gap. At present new resources are being offered and new partners recognized. We will attend to some of these and then return to the congregation.

Some Caring Practices in Ethical Discernment

Recognizing the many partners who participate in caring practices at the end of life, Duke University, through its seminary and medical school, offers workshops. The participants of these interdisciplinary workshops reflect on ethical issues of access to care and the quality of life to be available while one is dying. New conversations about prevention of pain and palliative care provide frameworks for caring practices that once abandoned the dying to their pain and isolation. Public policy connections are noted, and it is intended that all who participate have voice and reflect together on understandings of what is good in relation to this issue.

Many ethical decisions arise in terms of beginning and end of life issues. Practices in relation to unwanted pregnancies continue to fragment communities. In other places, voices raise issues of assisted suicide, and whether or not the creature can die on its own terms. Pastors need to participate in workshops and continuing education about these matters, and realize that many of the laity are already there, as physicians and nurses, hospital technicians of various sorts, and trained ethicists in a variety of faith traditions.

It is in this area of ethics that the challenge to receive changes in scientific and technological thinking is the most direct. While those experiencing chronic illness, such as Michael J. Fox, are pushing these boundaries, there is deep division between some theologians and some scientists when there is talk about the desirability of prolonging life. This issue of care is on the horizon between congregational and public discourse.

At a recent conference, scientists projected the possibility of a greater life span, arising from discoveries about stem cells and genetic manipulation. We are reminded of our own reflections about death in the first essay. Would human life be better off without death? Is the search for a longer life span a search for immortality and the inordinately powerful desire to be God?

Parishioners are already reading about cloning and gene manipulation, and making their own decisions (hopefully with the help of physician and chaplain) in relation to experimental treatments. Surely the creature's faith community should be present here.

Another shift from focus upon individual psychotherapy to placing the issues of care in broad interdisciplinary cultural context is the research coming out of The Family Project at the University of Chicago. Intentionally seeking to call forth a liberal Protestant voice in public discourse about family issues, Don Browning (1997) and his colleagues have offered opportunity for new reflections upon the definitions, goals, and processes of family life. If marriage intends children, then parental sacrifice is a value during the period that they need family care. This marriage should be one of mutuality and equal regard, modeling a style of partnership that needs to be modeled throughout a culture of domination and inequality. All are invited to the dialogue; as centers of moral discourse, congregations need to participate as they shape their family ministries and define who, for them, is indeed a family. The caring practices of family ministry occur with values that often seem self-evident and have not been lifted up for critical ethical reflection. The counseling of families or their members is fraught with ethical issues, not a simple matter of support or advocacy. On what basis are such counseling practices made?

All pastoral care includes moral perspectives, and yet there is little dialogue in seminaries between the disciplines of pastoral care and ethics. One of the strengths of current pastoral care could be to reach out to chaplains who practice in major medical centers, who are experienced in ways of thinking through complex moral decisions. Unlike many congregations, the thinking through there will lead to an immediate decision that will carry consequences. Hospital chaplains and ethics committees have developed resources for such deliberate inquiries and actions; it is time they are made available to seminarians so that they might teach them within congregations.

Some Considerations in the Ethics of Care

My earlier definition of care as a dimension of being human rather than as demanding professional certification is itself an ethical statement. The entirely beautiful creature, created in the image of God, is expected and able to offer its care to other creatures. When it does not, the others die, whether of physical or emotional neglect in the case of the infant and fragile elderly, or of being made voiceless and invisible, anonymous faces, as in the case of excluding or otherwise abusing others.

Mutuality attends perspectives on care. The developmentally disabled person is also a moral creature who, within his or her own level of functioning, can learn to live with and care for others. The disturbed adolescent, living in a psychiatric facility or a residential treatment center, will have houseparents, psychiatrists, social workers, psychologists, etc., but will also be expected to participate in his or her healing and reconciling processes—indeed, to care for others (peers) even as learning how to receive care. To not be viewed as capable of caring for another is to rob that person of humanity. Without at all diminishing the importance of specialized knowledge, an affirmation of the mutuality of care grounds our understanding of human being, along with its status as finite, limited, historical, relational and communal. As finite, it shares a vulnerability with other creatures that establishes mutuality; as relational an interdependence is present from the very beginning.

Related to mutuality, the moral perspective of equality grounds moral discourse. As many voices as possible are to be included in the dialogue. Within the restrictions imposed by law— that is, a boundary of legal age—young people should participate in decisions about their own care side by side with parents and other adults. The decision about amputation or disfiguring rotation of a leg affects the fourteen-year-old boy's future more than it does his parents. In the hospital context, recognition of mutuality and equal regard bring to the decision-making table nurses and pediatric care specialists, parents, physicians, and lawyers. In that setting there can be no imposed moral authority; there may even be quite different points of view about treatment; issues attending finality; and matters of time, money, and other resources.

In the present context that includes complex issues of globalization, pluralism, and violence, along with developments in science and technology, ethicists are focusing on the Christian's responsibility to receive the stranger, to embrace the other, and to refuse retaliation. These conversations need to be a dimension of the caring practices of every congregation, where they arise in the ordinary negotiations of determining policies, planning education, using mission funds, and quite simply relating to one another. As therapists have engaged in lengthy conversation with clients about their narratives and the ways that they intersect with their daily living, so might pastoral care persons be helpful in facilitating informed conversation about difficult issues in the congregation. Perhaps for seminarians there could be a clinical placement within an ecumenical or interfaith dialogue group, or supervision in facilitating the kind of listening and conversations that have informed those movements for the past fifty years. After all, serious theorists such as Volf contend that the issues of the relations between identity and diversity, between exclusion and embrace, are determinative of human values in our emerging world.

Another model is one in which persons with many different moral positions are intentionally called together to listen to each other without taking any votes. Examples could be a conference on issues of unwanted pregnancies with persons representing a continuum of views; or an interfaith dialogue on the death penalty including murder victim's families who are both anti- and pro-death penalty, attorneys for death row inmates, and death row clergy conversing with representatives of Christian, Islamic, and Jewish faiths. Caring for a variety of persons, perspectives, and institutions is carried in one community's purpose: We agree to differ. We promise to love. We unite to serve.

But whether concerned with determining an understanding of God's final ends (always risky) or at least being able to connect with them in making the kinds of decisions that shape immediate experience, pastoral care and moral discourse are totally entwined. A new set of resources about virtue, character, and responsibility might accompany more traditional resources that focus on development, feelings, and self-determination.

Once again we find that these conversations entail theological perceptions that may not be apparent at first glance. On the one hand, Christianity is an ethical religion, and looks to what can be determined from the practices of Jesus to mold an ethical code. "What Would Jesus Do?" is the concern within liberal and conservative churches, although their interpretations and prescribed practices may differ. Care seeks to meet the creature's needs, not only for food and shelter, but for love, justice, and belonging.

On the other hand, some regard the practices of care as revelatory events, pointing to the redemptive resources of Spirit and christology so that acts of care intend moral actions but also, in some way, disclose the presence and grace of God. Care practitioners have probably not sufficiently pondered these differences. After all, the goal is to guide the creature in making nuanced and informed moral judgments on its situation of perennial peril and moral dilemmas.

We will return to this issue as I later present definitions of pastoral care that include both perspectives. Pastoral care is faithful living by finite creatures in their particular historical contexts. And pastoral care bears witness to the possibilities of experiencing joy and the goodness of God…even in these places.[1]

---

[1]At one point in the history of pastoral care, discipline was a caring practice; related to moral guidance it determined the boundaries of community participation in receiving the sacraments and other blessings. In another place than this, pastoral care needs to reflect on any emerging expectations of "right living" that would be authoritative, exceptions to which would carry banishment, i.e., incest, priestly abuse of children and young people, etc. In many ways conversations about the recent scandals in the Roman Catholic Church have been about the practices of discipline and care.

Public Discourse, Care, and Culture

PROMOTING CREATURELY WELL-BEING

Conversations about care—and pastoral care—lead inevitably to the public arena and understandings about the relationships between church and culture. The nature and practices of care are issues for the public domain, where shared partnerships carry responsibility for its public and private embodiments.

Congregations do not always understand this.

As Professor Martin Marty pointed out, the average person relates to religion not as a source of strife, but as a quiet, healing force personified by the pastor who reconciles a divorcing couple, or the chaplain who delivers last rites to the dying. We're seeing now that religion is not an innocent force in the world, but that it shares in the same problems as the rest of the world.

The church itself is an institution that is one voice in the cultural networks of care. Not only do its caring practices serve civil society, but what is going on in the culture can profoundly alter ecclesial practices. One example is the way in which federal and state legislation affected church related institutions that served the developmentally disabled. Deinstitutionalization sought to bring a family value to placing persons with such conditions in group homes. Efforts to make churches and other religious institutions more accessible were stimulated by federal legislation, although they had sought and received exclusion from it. A memorable picture for UCC readers of this essay is that of Harold Wilke, who lived a life as a church leader without arms, signing the Americans with Disabilities Act document.

The many ramifications of church/state or church/culture or religion/society issues are not our concern here. The focus is how these grounding understandings affect conversations about care. As we begin, three interpretations may be helpful.

First, religion is a social force with vitality and responsibility for culture. Its power is intentionally controlled within Western democracies because different religions—or even faith groups—at various points within the historical process may claim to speak for God and be responsible for the civil order and governmental processes. Conversations about care will find this an active tension even in the United States. How are persons with unwanted pregnancies to be cared for? What are the civil rights and cultural norms affecting gay and lesbian couples in regard to their desire to adopt children who would not otherwise find a home? How are the prescription needs of the elderly to be cared for through the Medicare and Medicaid systems? Here the deep connections between particularity in ecclesial situations of ministries with the fragile elderly, for example, connect directly with issues of public discourse. So does legislation controlling the quality of care in nursing homes, and a local church's position on just salaries for attendants when a strike is threatened at a local facility. Indeed, such may force a congregation to look at its own pay scale for secretarial, custodial, and daycare employees!

Second, the concept of culture carries within itself vitalities and positive sensibilities about care. Secular institutions need not be less caring than religious ones! Meland's understandings are helpful. The streams of experience that carry the history, felt memories, and embodied forms of that which has been valued by religious groups have also found their way into the secular world. Values of individualism and hard work, fears of punishment for sin, hoped for reconciliation with the departed, the right not to be oppressed by religious or sectarian institutions—each of these and many more are carried deeply within the culture's values about care. We recall that Meland posits three witnesses to the faith: the witness of the individual, the witness of the cultus or church, and the witness of the culture, which cannot be neatly separated from its religious shapings in the past. The perspectives of the pilgrims and the colonists, the evangelists and those in the social gospel movement, live on in fragments and practices, residual values and points of view.

Caregivers listening to teenagers in residential treatment centers will hear stories about expectations of punishment or hope from neglected or abused persons who have never set foot within a church. They may wear crosses and draw pictures with religious themes. Atheists may forget that their expectation of freedom from religious orthodoxy is itself a complicated gift from religious movements that themselves had sought freedom from a prescribed perspective!

Third, experiences with the needs for, and practices of, care in both ecclesial and secular settings disclose the present workings out in history of the emergent themes of the twenty-first century. We have already noted how new knowledge and claims within science and technology have stated new ethical concerns in the hospital, where private and public are inexorably connected. Fundamentalists may participate in new technologies when their own caring needs are at stake, especially within the particularities of their own families.

In public settings, different religious groups whose understandings may be totally incommensurable will reflect differing values about care. "Right to die," "no extreme measures," and "God alone decides when death shall occur" will traffic together in the same institution, sometimes within the same family. Planned Parenthood will be threatened with the loss of public funds when it seeks to extend care to those inquiring about birth control or abortion; persons who speak for prisoners, guards, families of prisoners, families of their victims, voices for and against capital punishment from within differing religious groups—all these will converse together. As suggested previously, the chaplains who serve at such intersections of public and private may be the best pastoral care teachers in preparing for future caring ministries in such areas. Another set of public/private resources can be found in the newer agencies that have sought to offer care to populations experiencing domestic violence, dealing with the manifold embodiment of the HIV virus, seeking all-options counseling for unwanted pregnancies, and so on. Here religion and culture cooperate in care.

Pastors as Public Persons...Members of the Laity as Citizens

The intimate connections between church and the public sector in the areas of care are not always recognized. Within the United Church of Christ, a lawyer who has spent forty-five years in faith-based human services reports these startling statistics:

According to the UCC, in 2003, operating budgets of 341 agencies in the UCC's Council of Health and Human Service Ministries totaled $3.6 billion, the charitable contributions accounting for $28 million (about three-quarters of one percent).

Most of the $3.6 billion came from federal, state, and local governments through Medicare, Medicaid, Social Security, TANF (Temporary Assistance for Needy Families, replacing AFDC—Aid to Families with Dependent Children), and other tax-based programs. UCC Health and Human Service Ministries would dry up, were it not for the taxing authority of government. The lack of contact between pastoral care ministries and the denomination's own networks of care has contributed to a lack of realistic perspective. The health care agencies of any denomination are not primarily identified with religious psychotherapy services or professional pastoral counseling, although, of course, they utilize the resources of psychologists, social workers, psychiatrists, and so on, as they enhance their particular programming area. Within denominations such as the United Church of Christ, national energies have frequently seemed to focus around liberation issues, to a diminishment of concern in the care giving offered in residential treatment centers, hospitals and retirement centers, urban ministry programs, group care for the developmentally disabled, and so forth. The umbrella of care has not been big enough to include the creatures' many needs for care and the many caring partners who participate. Theologically, the quality of care offered the frail elderly person who is incontinent and bedridden is as important as the care accorded groups of persons through embrace rather than exclusion. In other words, theologically, the embodiment of (and economic support for) little kindnesses is of as much cultural value as freeing the oppressed, and may indeed be even more demanding of the creature's full participation in the process. Anna Quindlen (2002) may unintentionally help us see this through her essay about her son's birthday falling on September 11. She needed a double vision to see both horror and joy, and to invest in whatever she could do in relation to future acts of terror at the same time as she celebrated her gratitude for her relationship with her son. As we will see, this capacity to lean both ways with integrity is crucial in the ability to experience joy and gratitude.

There are, of course, pastoral care literatures that suggest connections and provide frameworks for social justice ministries within the perspectives of the discipline. The concern here is more with congregations, who, as the earlier quote from Martin Marty and the report from the United Church of Christ suggest, may not have claimed—or known how to claim—their intrinsic connectedness with the particular cultures in which they are located. A report from Hartford Seminary is included here in order to illustrate this:

Congregations Serve as Beacons of Hope

They are beacons of hope everywhere. They are houses of worship in every corner of the U.S. providing assistance to individuals and families through hard times, especially in sudden emergencies. And that included a growing number of mosques well before the September 11 terrorist attacks thrust U.S. Muslim communities into the spotlight.

In this nearly universal practice of caring, congregations with widely different beliefs and from many locations respond in moments of need, with cash (88 percent) and food (85 percent) the most frequent responses. Clothing, shelter, medical attention and crisis counseling follow in that order... Also, in last year's study of 14,301 congregations by Faith Communities Today (FACT), almost nine out of ten congregations reported that they serve as the last resort for neighbors in need.

Among ministries of care, senior citizen programs proved to be most common at 45 percent, but about a third of these churches, synagogues and mosques also support ministries in day care, tutoring literacy and health programs. In these ministries, volunteers are more likely than in the emergency programs to get to know the people they are serving.

A smaller but still significant number of congregations engaged in reform-seeking social ministries...Such programs involved cooperative efforts with other churches, organized by trained leaders and supported by volunteers.

Muslim mosques, or masjids, exhibit the same high level of community caring as the churches and synagogues down the street. With the FACT data, the Council on American-Islamic Relations shows what mosques assist families and individuals with cash (90 percent), counseling or food (both 77 percent), prison or jail programs (66 percent) and clothing (64 percent). These typically higher rates of support reflect a deep commitment to helping people get a foothold in society. (Dudley, 2002, 20)

Little attention is paid in seminaries to the pastor as a public person who will perennially be caught up in church-state issues. Should they pray at local football games? How can they guide congregations concerning the placement of the American flag in sanctuaries? Where are ordinary caregivers lifted up for praise, that is, front line staff in hospitals, nursing homes, and so forth? How does the local church express its own theology of mutuality and equal regard in establishing salary guidelines for childcare workers? How are the members of the congregation who are asked to serve on boards of church-related social welfare organizations guided to understand their crucial theological—and not simply economic—role? How do local church educational programs help parishioners understand changes within the various public systems that affect them so that they do not experience shock (as many did) when confronted with the need for signatures on "do not resuscitate" orders, or the movement of one of their adult children with Down's from a relatively safe institutional setting to a group home in an urban setting?

This huge network of partners in caring processes includes laity as citizens. Embodying their own sense of call or vocation, they operate both within professional guidelines *and* the understandings of their faith. They will be present where pastors do not go, and will be the voice of theology in strange places where salaries are negotiated, access issues debated, funding resources sought. Yom Kippur can be understood as a religious event that brings together life's unpredictability and human frailty. This religious understanding is also one that can help to interpret the courage of ordinary secular caregivers such as ambulance attendants and representatives of the police and fire departments, who need preparation and after care for the caring services that they offer. Certainly they deal with life's unpredictability and human frailties!

A dramatic form of this follows: Someone has to mark and pick up the body parts after an air, terrorist attack, flood, or traffic disaster. In the military, the lowest echelon troops are trained to do this, by carefully staking out and walking through fields where pieces of chickens have been scattered to represent the body parts—and their smell. These folk may be parts of medical rescue teams, trained disaster teams, or members of the National Guard. Surely they qualify to be participants in the cultural networks of care, and it is hoped that their stories—and their needs—are included in theological conversations about pastoral care. It is the chaplains who follow them and attend to their emotions.

Guides for Enactment

A helpful theological orientation when pondering the immensity of the tasks of offering care in a pluralistic culture is one of recognizing that the visions are not the given but the task. So has it always been. The world cannot be made to start over. Nor can the form of society that God prefers be simply announced and applied. Pastoral care already knows this if it has reflected deeply enough on its experiences with the creatures' various finitudes and limitations. Even the best religious psychotherapy that brings about change in a confused identity happens only slowly and over time. Shifts in family dynamics do not immediately happen, even with Rabbi Edward Friedman's parabolic gifts; and the complicated processes of calling forth community continue not only in local congregations but in all governmental processes. This is, indeed, the human situation.

We are not left forsaken at the immensity of the task. We begin by appreciating the many partners and being open to learning from one another. This commitment to shared knowledge can guide our learnings interprofessionally and in terms of ecumenical/interfaith dialogue. In many settings our guides become our chaplains; the caring work done in the military can guide us in deeper understandings of class differences, as well as the possibilities of fundamentalists and

Presbyterians, Sikhs and Mormons, and rabbis from all three Jewish traditions being able to plan and work together.

Yet another set of guides could be experienced pastoral psycho-therapists adept at listening to a variety of stories. Transferring and adapting those skills to the styles of civil conversations necessary to better meet the need of the creatures in a civic society would be a real caring contribution. Hopefully, congregations such as my church in Tennessee will experience what it is like to have open dialogue with friends and find ways of remaining together; this may be an ecclesial gift to the secular community.

As congregations and denominations experience their own styles of greeting incommensurable differences, the learnings might be translated through the laity into various civic groups of associations that are ethnically integrated. Ashutosh Varshney (1995, 2002), a political scientist at the University of Michigan, found that such organizations were an effective way of controlling conflict when it broke out in urban settings. As he studied violence in riot-prone cities where Hindu/Muslim rioting was endemic, he discovered a clear pattern: "cities with developed social, political and economic integration were far less vulnerable to conflict." The ethnically integrated organizations that he studied included business organizations, trade unions, professional groups, political parties, sports clubs. If societies are to manage diversity—both so that violence does not break out, and so that they can work together on issues of care—there needs to be a place where many voices can help to stem the tide of violence. While the Varshney model is not reflected here, it is probable that pre-existing groups where interfaith dialogue had been a reality were helpful in interpreting the events of September 11 and helping to prevent the spread of rumor, misunderstandings, and new urban myths. In a world of violence and terrorism such groups care for the cultural fabric.

The work by Martin Marty mentioned earlier may be helpful. Some of the perspectives of pastoral care may carry too idealistic understandings of the integrities and intimacies needed for the development of human community. Perhaps some forms of community are restricted to more intimate and intentional settings, like biological or extended family and congregation. The slow development of mutual respect and tolerance across boundary lines in various forms of associations may be as effective agents of care in this area of faith and culture intersection than the expectation of more intimate communities with persons of shared values. Frequently a liberal perspective has anticipated that others will be assimilated into that value system. This expectation does not take difference seriously enough.

In any event, family, congregation (synagogue/mosque), and broader governmental communities are in the business of calling forth community (or healthy associations) and engaging in moral discourse on behalf of creaturely well-being.

Further guides in these caring processes are leaders such as Thomas Groome (1991) and Don Browning (1983), whose work in the area of practical theology combines a concern for both the particularity of care and its connections to public policy. Both are clear about connections between faith and culture. Groome says it well: there is no Christianity without culture, and no culture without religion. And Browning builds in the ethical search for what is best for the creature (or at least better) in pondering issues of marriage and family life, the raising of children, the formulation of public policies regarding family life, and the competing secular/religious/theological voices and systems of truth that seek to participate in the wide-reaching dialogues that relate cultural movements toward what is most efficacious in family ministries. As we look ahead, it is probable that there will be more persons with doctorates in practical theology emerging in the next five years than in pastoral counseling. A recent conference in Nashville included all of its participants in formulating a practical theology of cancer. The Lilly Endowment has recently funded Candler/Emory for the preparation of forty such persons over the next five years. Pastors and laity who continue to define pastoral care and pastoral practices only in terms of the psychological and individual orientation of the pastoral care discipline will be missing a real opportunity to connect the church's caring practices with emerging cultural developments. Once, the margins of the field were the study of developmental thought, personality theory, and a clinical focus. These foci continue to be irreplaceable—but within a larger framework of what care means culturally, ethically, and theologically, as well as within many modes and contexts.

A final comment: when the church is viewed as an institution within the larger cultural network of care, three considerations emerge. First, there are public issues of accountability and excellence in the provision of service and management of funds. Expect negotiation. Second, it is preferable for a theological view of social institutions to view them positively rather than negatively. This does not mean that they are not regularly to be subjected to critique. But cynicism and disdain toward institutions frequently reveals as much about the critic as about the nature of institutions themselves. Institutions are functionally a way of caring for the creatures' needs and, though they may become oppressive, but that is not their intent, and those disdainful of the positive value of cultural institutions are naïve.

Third, as a caring institution, the institution itself frequently requires care, perhaps a check up on the functioning of its bodily parts (occurring through denominational resources or groups such as the Alban Institute). Or it may need the healing of memories after a pastoral abuse situation that was never directly discussed. It may need hospice care when it is dying or guidance in making decisions about its future. Like a family, there may be an elephant lying in the middle of the congregation that prevents it from getting on with its tasks as the body of Christ, calling forth community and moral discourse, and itself becoming a place where the creature can count on being received with hospitality and care.

The Creature as Relational, Communal, Moral

We have now named the human creature as finite, limited, historical, and vulnerable; and as relational, communal, moral, and with a public face. These various shocks of finitude limitation and otherness are intrinsic in the human situation and the many modes of pastoral care that attend them. They are so persistent as to focus conversations about care on suffering, not joy, and so problematic as to focus understandings of God on theodicy and sin, not the goodness of either God or the created human creature—but more of that in movement 3.

In movement 2, I have described some of the situations and tasks of pastoral care in the vast area of identity and community, and their ethical and moral dimensions, in order to make several theological points about pastoral care interpretations and practices.

First, in accepting Volf's reading of the issues of identity and community (embrace and exclusion) as central issues for the community of faith, I am claiming that pastoral care perspectives and practices can make a positive contribution. Through understandings of identity development (developmentalism, personality theory, systems theory, etc.) pastoral care practitioners contribute regularly to the formation of identities that can not only stand to live with others, but can reach out to embrace others. Practices of identity formation in congregational or therapeutic settings, through worship or educational experiences, can make a direct contribution to understanding, in particular, situations concerning how creatures actually do learn to receive and embrace those who have been viewed not only as strangers, but as *dangerous* strangers. When pastoral care expands its perspectives to include participation in interfaith civic groups that seek peace and understanding, they contribute to a culture of care in which violence can, perhaps, at least be mitigated. Even more important, creatures are formed who understand that the world is so vast in its pluralism and global orientations that the tasks of care are intrinsic and not accidental, perennial and not problems to be solved. Creatures can affirm that they have only margins of intelligibility, as positive, not negative assessment of their creaturely stance.

Pastoral care's turn to the hermeneutics of story and narrative, whether expressed in personal sharing; family narratives; or the tales of a congregation, denomination, or nation, can be useful in recognizing—and perhaps limiting—how narratives of hatred and estrangement are also carried deeply within the tales. Rage and hatred of named oppressors linger and fester in individual, tribal, and national consciousness. Some of these malignancies appear less lethal than others in a democratic society, where there is less concern for issues related to class, the result being that churches fail to reach out and include persons marked by histories of poverty and exclusion, low-wage jobs without job security, marginal wages, and so on. This becomes a subtle edge of discrimination and failure in mutual regard, embodied in denominational demographics. Congregations might be intentionally shaped to practice and learn how to let go of such potentially divisive imaging...for they fester when unnamed, and even when not mentioned infect the denominational and body politic as there are tensions and needs for calmness in the midst of violence. And, unwittingly, they are carried by us all.

It may well be that some of pastoral care's concerns with deep listening, the capacity to distance oneself enough to hear more accurately, the attempt not to have the self get in the way of the other's needs, might model the practices necessary for civil discourse in a fractured public world. It certainly does not help when religions join the fray, all too often living out their own history of violence in the name of the God that they think they fully understand. For others, the disdain experienced toward those with the wrong God—or political point of view—carries its own dynamics of exclusion and failure to embrace.

Such issues hover within and around all of the practices of pastoral care. As there is no mind/body split, so is there no neat categorization of acts of care from acts of justice, or of concern for the particular leaving out the broader issues—or vice versa. We are, of course, speaking within a theological orientation that trusts that, for the Christian, living in the midst of an historical faith and one in which God chose to enter and live among us, ultimacy and immediacy traffic together. Christian care is neither an application of so-called Christian doctrines or principles; nor is it immersion in one particularity, or a refusal to bear witness to the truths of the faith in ways that not only connect with the situation, but rise up and dwell within it.

Finally, the issues of movement 2, even more deeply than those of the first movement, require ways to perceive culture that are as open to benevolence as to malevolence, as open to the workings of providence as they are determined to describe a universe empty of mystery and grace, as willing to celebrate the resources of culture as they are to name the demons that dwell deeply within. These essays reject John Baille's thesis that culture is founded on violence, and that its preservation has been secured through scapegoating, although the argument is tempting. It ends, however, as it must, with a christology necessary to save the world from itself. It is interesting to find authors such as Maureen Dowd frequently writing in similar fashion, that all is corrupt and oppressive: governments and scientists, politicians and priests. But the view undergirding the essays in this book intentionally seeks to avoid the identification of history itself with evil or, for that matter, of finitude being a condition of punishment for which the creature must continually blame God— or spend decades of tormented thought processes to explain God, protect God, take care of God, if you will.

Movement 3 now turns to the project of defining the practices of pastoral care as witnessing to the joy that the creature is promised, and witnessing to the goodness of the God who created creatures and placed, not threw, us into an always undulating world of elements and dynamics, forces and counterforces—a pulsating temporality, if you will, filled with awe and the awful.

About Hope and Possibilities

Joy and the Goodness of God

The following four essays are about words seldom talked about in the pastoral care literatures, that is, joy, the goodness of God, the peace that passes understanding, and play. They include comments upon the formation of those who offer care in this mode, and the special knowledges required.

This movement intends to invite conversation about defining pastoral care as acts of compassion that witness to joy and the goodness of God in the problematic and perilous moments within human history where ultimacy and immediacy meet…and the human creature experiences the persistent and perennial shocks of finitude, limitation, and otherness…

The move to this place through experiences of searing loss, horrendous evil, the devastation of shattered expectations, and irreconcilable differences that carry perennial estrangements and permanent rage or melancholy has been intentional. It is hard for guilty persons to experience joy; for persons experiencing shame to trust another's acceptance; for those enraged by loss or oppression to give or receive the graces of forgiveness; for those with weak egos to receive strangers; and those with powerful egos to receive God.

The decision to begin with the pains, puzzlements, and perils of the creature's situation was done so that the move toward celebration could be made from the depths. Joy cannot be experienced until one has incorporated pain—or perhaps until one can understand that sometimes one's joy is the simultaneous occasion for another's grief, as in the relationship between organ receiver and the family of the donor. Or until one can realize that the experience of joy in one place may be simultaneous with the experience of devastation in another. And the goodness of God stands in question—to be pondered in abstractions by theologians and philosophers down through the centuries—if it is a principle that must be logically derived, a concept that must be rigidly applied, or a verse on a Hallmark card that is so thin that it has led to trivializing sentiment and negating those who have not pondered such issues. For God's goodness must be a reality that is deeply experienced and claimed. The two preceding movements all too often force one to become God's apologist, or advocate, or perhaps defense lawyer! Especially when theorists intentionally or unintentionally fall into the trap of identifying finitude (or history) itself as evil (or sin), there is no place to go for a pastoral care that wants to celebrate joy and goodness. Also to be valued are the creature's experiences of benevolence as well as malevolence; the creative resources that technology has offered to help the blind navigate, the deaf hear, the paralyzed move, the paraplegic have hope; and the possibility of "good deaths" through communal palliative care, and the refusal to abandon the elderly and dying. Sustained interfaith dialogue, meaningful sacrifice freely lifted up for another, the availability of care givers embodying compassion in their own ways throughout social structures, racial and ethnic gatherings, little movements toward greater inclusiveness and embrace, little movements away from exclusion, and, above all, little kindnesses…each of these witnesses to possibility, joy, and goodness.

But for the case to be made, controversial issues must be engaged, and they will be throughout the presentation of the following essays. We will seek to find God in the depths of history and culture itself, not only a God of tenderness and mercy, luring the creatures toward fulfillment, but also grounded in some semblance of ontic truth. Truly it is good that we have discovered God as a fellow sufferer; truly it is not sufficient to have there be no left over or more of God to invite the sufferer to live on toward new blessings. The size of God does matter.

It will be important to argue against John Baille that violence is the ordering principle of culture, which is why it was crucial to begin with devastation and destruction. But his narrow understanding of the complexities of culture, and his discovery of a root metaphor that, in his judgment, explains everything, are not helpful to a pastoral care that views human culture with more gracious eyes and seeks to present no single metaphor to ease the suffering of the creatures. It is probable that if history and culture themselves are evil and grounded in violence, that there can be no substitute for a God who insists on the rigid application of "his" own power to make any difference. And we have already been there.

In addition, we will have to look at ego in relation to both God and violence, finding it necessary for the one who would experience the goodness of God not to consider oneself already God. Differentiation between wish and hope is necessary; a threatened ego blames God when it does not get its own way, or when life is discovered to be unfair. Since only the mature ego can courageously exist at the same time as it receives finitude and limitation, irreconcilable differences and the requirement for continual alerts in ethical dialogue and public formation of systems that are good enough can be endured. Theologies that posit anxiety and the need to secure the self may not have benefited from reactions of gratitude, joy, and praise, as well as anxiety and possibilities of the self-finding itself in relationships with the many creatures with whom a cosmos is shared.

The central question of pastoral care is probably: Why did God do this to me? Within this movement we will approach the question from different points of view from that of theodicy and the presence of a suffering God, without negating their healing role in the human pilgrimage and interpretive power with those needing care.

But the central issue has to be the placement of the good God at the center of it all, Creator, Redeemer, Judge, choosing the self-limitation of working through the processes of history and culture, human development and the formation of human community, to usher in the realm that the creatures have heard promised in their visions and the various streams of experience in which they have been born.

For creatures *are* finite, limited, and historical and are so created—determined in many ways, trapped in peril and vulnerability. Even their real freedom is impaired, as existence has been wrought out, not given. They are also in a continual process of identity and community formation, grounded in biochemical and social psychological economic dynamics. They are deeply cultural and intrinsically decisional/moral, yet continually open to the shocks of finitude and otherness!

But they are also created out of a love that is joyful, by a Goodness whose goodness and mystery is inexhaustible and more profound than the mysteries of evil, and they can and have experienced moments or intimations of peace within themselves and their complex relationships with other creatures and their God. And they are playful, embodied in their very developmental pilgrimage, playful as they learn about their contexts. It is important that that playfulness find a matching metaphor in one of the dimensions of the Creator God— at play with a sense of spontaneity and future, possibility and new learning. Let us note that play is forbidden in autocratic cultures, controlled where patriarchy reigns, and the playfulness of oppressed peoples must be carefully watched by the oppressor.

Thus the concluding essays are about joy, goodness, peace, and play, and define pastoral care as bearing witness to joy and the goodness of God.

The Shocks of Finitude and the Joy and Goodness of God

To Make Connection

We begin by making connection...How are we to move from the historical reality of the manifold, perennial, and perilous shocks of finitude to experiences of authentic joy and the goodness of God? Let us begin by reflecting theologically; in terms of definitions of pastoral care that intrinsically relate its practices to those of worship and ritual; on the need for renewed exploration of human religious experiencing in the contemporary world; and by a turn to liberation thought.

For the Christian, *joy* is irrevocably connected to God, whether the transcendent God of classical thought or the God whose ultimate and immediate natures traffic together. For these are the connections of finitude and limitation in their manifold forms with their Creator and perennial presence in creaturely existence. The disciples are afraid—*and* are filled with joy. The crucifixion not only connects death with life's ongoingness, but presents the everydayness of a Saturday that connects the two...even as the Monday following Easter leads immediately into a continuation of the ordinary workings of historical existence.

Sacramental celebrations intentionally connect finitude with its deeper meanings when placed within the arms of God. Whether there are two sacraments or seven, the human life cycle is permeated with occasions that recognize the coming together of human problematics with God's possibilities. The knowledge that God loves us makes our joy complete. Our personal stories—and family, community, or cultural narratives—are to become connected (or reconnected) to God's story, the story and narrative of divine power and presence in relation to creaturely existence.

In their contemporary forms, the stories of pastoral care have been more connected with psychological understandings than with theology. In various ways, the shocks of finitude have been addressed by therapeutic orientations, conflict management techniques, various systems theories, diagnostic perspectives carrying within them expectations of cure, growth therapies, and so forth. At one point, several therapeutic modalities were described as carrying a culture of joy, which was negatively critiqued by theologian/ethicist Don Browning (1980), who found within it deep antipathy to human finitude, a romantic view of the individual when free to define his or her own existence without cultural impediments, the refusal of any authority beyond the self, and a naive expectation that, left alone, human beings would make right choices (within one system of thought, even of the foods that the infant would choose to eat!)

Along with the intentional theological connection in seeking to move authentically from the shocks of finitude to joy and the goodness of God, the move made by Anderson and Foley in defining pastoral care in relation to its place in relation to worship and ritual making needs to be affirmed. In their perspective, both the visions and the problematics of human experience can come together in making intentional connections between story and ritual. For, using John Dominic Crossan (Anderson & Foley, 1997; Crossan, 1975), ritual includes both the parabolic (within which my perspectives on finitude are carried) and the mythic (within which visions of fulfillment and hopeful expectations are carried).

Thus, as these essays turn toward a definition of pastoral care as witnessing to the joy and goodness of God, they find solid grounding in theology's many connections in dealing with such issues. Similar connections lie within the ecclesial community—the churches— where the stories of God's love carry the stories of Christ's death, and the stories of liberation from Pharaoh carry the reality of not getting to the promised land. In local churches, the intent to be a caring community of equality and grace carries within it historical, cultural, and theological impediments. Indeed, local churches may be the only place within our culture where lament and praise, gratitude and sorrow, grief and joy, limitation and boundary breaking find common ground.

A third connection lies within renewed attention to contemporary religious experience, almost totally neglected since William James. Pruyser, as a contemporary person competent in the psychology of religion, broke new ground in connection to the practice of ministry, with the turn from primarily psychological categories to define the mentally ill toward attempts to invite theological diagnoses. Nancy Ramsay's (1998) recent work carries this into the mainstream of pastoral care practices, where listening for understandings of God, grace, communion, providence, and so on, in the stories of our parishioners, clients, and patients, enriches both our understandings of them and the way in which we might see them differently. A very perceptive first-year seminarian student writes of the ways in which ritual and theological understandings might reinvent a liberal Protestantism's mission with the abandoned young people who populate residential treatment centers. Their religious experiences, as well as their needs for coauthorship of their stories and rituals to help them make meaning, including rituals that take seriously the painful and abusive experiences of their lives, have not been a dimension of their therapies. Perhaps this well states pastoral care's historic turn from its own foundations, and its apparent voicelessness in caring for the growing numbers of abandoned children and young people in our culture, even within the church's own social welfare institutions.

There is a fourth connection between the shocks of finitude that I have described and a pastoral care viewed as witnessing to joy and the goodness of God. That lies within liberation thought, beginning, perhaps, with the Old Testament, where the folk counted on God to be a part of their story within their political history, and to liberate them from its oppressive dimensions. Some liberationists have noted how oppressive regimes seek to control play, as its spontaneity threatens established order and the official meaning given to human stories. Or the stories of the oppressed shout an alternative to the official cultural stories—and their stories carry within joy and hope.

A feminist ethic gives equal weighting to the importance of resisting, persisting, and celebrating, as well as to the capacity for the oppressed to dare to name the workings of the Divine in the midst of their oppression and, hence, to place the shocks of finitude in perspectives that carries not only future meaning but the very presence of God within them. Thus joy can abound—even there!

The move from the shocks/realities of both biological and historical finitude and limitation is, therefore, a process rather than a leap, the claiming of deeper realities rather than the refusal of depths in the name of cure or fix or simple understanding, whether of individual salvation or a particular political platform.

An Overview of Scriptural Perspectives on Joy

Here I seek to make further connections between joy and selected scriptural values. I want to invite discussion, not present resolution; suggest some topics for conversation, not define the most important ones; and approach the topic through the familiar, rather than new conceptualities. Further, I present these concepts negatively: One *cannot* find *joy* if one seeks to be God; cannot celebrate little kindnesses; cannot affirm that everyone counts; and cannot seek to have everyone eat. In other words, here I will speak of what gets in the way of joy.

To experience joy, the human creature must claim one's creaturely stance and not seek to be God. The scripture most claimed by our students is one in which the love of justice and mercy also expects one to walk humbly *with* God, not to *be* God. Our care seeks to bind persons experiencing tribulation to a transcendent God, and/or to an ultimacy within particularity, but never to the agent of care. William James (2004) is quite clear that the human has no choice but to claim its "ontic dependency," in other words, to know it is not God. To help one take off the mantle of having to be God is a continuing issue of therapy and spiritual care, both of which seek to make easier what is in any case necessary, that is, to claim a creaturely stance.

As we shall see, a primary psychoanalytic point of view is that neurosis and joy are opposites. The affective state that requires control, i.e., to be God, has no energies left over to receive futures, to be open to the unexpected, to be surprised by joy! Even Henri Nouwen (1997), a Henri suspicious of joy, is surprised to find it in the L'Arche community, where he experiences the equality of brothers and sisters rather than the heavy authority of the priest, or the elitisms of Yale and Harvard. Again and again perspectives of spirituality and psychology of religion note the need to let go of ego in order to receive joy. For a field that has prided itself on growing, strengthening, or developing ego strength, this may appear as a perplexing message. But it relates to rejection of finitude and limitation of which perhaps only a healthy ego can afford to let go.

It is probable that the one who refuses the creaturely stance is also bereft of the capacity to celebrate little things, little kindnesses, small acts of tenderness, and ordinary gentleness. For we who would be God would right the world, begin it over, announce it as a place of equality and justice for all, make the big moves that would assure an end to war and violence, and pass the legislation that would immediately assure inclusion and eliminate the various "-isms." The continual frustrations of those who hate to live this side of the promised land prevent them from seeing and participating in the little connections that lie at the core of family and culture. For this focus on little things or kindnesses is also a focus on little people, those whose everyday living may be more determinative of the shape of human reality and cultural humaneness than those whose role is just as important but more up-front. We have previously noted how the more hands-on the care is that is offered in our culture, the less the caregiver is valued. This is the world of childcare and nursing homes, of hospice and everyday family evenings, of church potlucks and school carnivals, of not being faceless and anonymous in a world speeding by, of having someone to speak your name, and be glad you came. This, in turn, requires a move from focus on the macrocosmic world of "Big Things" and "Big Issues" to the microcosmic world of particularity and everyday embodiment. That is the primary world of pastoral care.

To move from the joy to be found in little things to the joy that is experienced when everyone counts is another move of authenticity. When scripture celebrates the many gifts, many of us do not see beyond the greater splendor of those who carry power and prestige, important names and positions. Yet the houseparents in the residential treatment center count as much as the social workers and psychiatrists in their ministries with abandoned youth, and a pleasant experience with a clerk may make one's day, while, simultaneously, neither to be seen nor heard by some social functionary may enhance the notion of not counting, which gets in the way of experiencing joy.

I have recently come across this simple poem that makes the case more profoundly than I can do, as it has to do with ways of seeing, places of meaning, simple presences that can carry joy.

Joy can lie in a glimpse of acute seeing…of noticing…

> Over the years, among the fallen, the survived,
> the mad, the helpless, the drunken, the unachieved,
> I see what it is to make a tiny flicker,
> a New England barn glimpsed in summer,
> a red sign rising among the green,
> like the cardinal posed on the bird feeder this morning,
> God knows between where and where, fall coming,
> winter about to sew its brutish cubes,
> and the cardinal here in its light landing.
>
> (Moss, 1995)

And there are places where, if we do not look carefully, we will not see…or if we do not allow for joy's presence everywhere, we will leave some places empty that might be carriers of joy…

While scripture may incline us to think of big things such as salvation, justice, peace, redemption, many of the actual workings of church and culture occur through little kindnesses. In one of the many stories coming out of the 9/11 events, it was reported that the owner of a florist shop that was devastated in its location near the Twin Towers told a story of her decision to remain. After she cleaned up her shop she filled it with joyful and aromatic flowers, a sign of hope. A customer came in and said, "I am not buying flowers. I just came in to celebrate a note of joy."

In scripture, everybody counts. They count because each of their gifts is important because each has been created in God's image; because through God's preference for the poor, everyone is given a place; because God invited everyone to the many banquets; because children have a place and the dying are cared for; because healing occurs, and the oppressed are liberated.

Christian joy is not possible unless everyone counts. To experience the reality of human belonging with others brings joy; to be able to see persons around you as children of God who count brings joy even as it diminishes one's sense of importance, control, and godlikeness. This is one of the many reasons why pastoral care participants report so often on feelings of joy when they deeply see others. As we shall see, the neurotic need for control of others and refusal to enter into relationships because of time pressures gets in the way of joy. Joy insists on openness...to little kindnesses, to seeing every person as one who counts, to acknowledging that one is not godlike in relationship with them, that is, playing that they are God.

Joy is also present when everyone eats. The focus on the story of the bread and fishes is not the miracle of feeding 5,000 (plus the women and children), but that everyone ate! The task is not to explain the miracle but to celebrate the possibility and commit oneself to the joyful possibility not only that everyone eats, but that everyone belongs—that every child has a warm winter coat—that every homeless person has a warm place to sleep on cold nights—that every family has a place to live in—that every abandoned child finds a place of belonging. That this does not happen can lead one to cynicism, which, as Henry Nouwen reminds us, is the opposite of joy. The opposite of joy is *not* realism—there is much to do, and many shocks of finitude and limitation, injustice and invisibility. But the tasks can be pursued in little ways with hope, blessing, and joy.

But, if the opposite of joy is cynicism, then there can be no joy found in sharing in the various disdains and impossibilities that prevent the tasks of joy—even as little kindnesses—from being carried out. Along with the connections made earlier, between the shocks of finitude and the authenticity of joy and goodness, lie these deceptively simple practices that refuse cynicism and impossibility. Human beings are not God, and when they claim or expect to be so, their disappointed expectations can lead to cynicism, contempt, hopelessness, withdrawal, the sourness of utopias unfulfilled. This diminishes the various practices of persistence that provide for care at the core of family, congregation, and culture, for little kindnesses count. Everybody—and their gifts—count. There is joy when everyone eats and the eaters take upon themselves the tasks of feeding and clothing, sheltering and caring for body, psyche and soul, even in their own places and contexts, even in the midst of the very shocks of finitude and limitation that accompany the creature in history.

Some Theological and Cultural Dynamics of Joy

The central issue in considering the dynamics of *joy* is the capacity of human religious experience to receive both awfulness and awe-fullness with authenticity. Pruyser (1976) speaks of the realities of the experience of benevolence *and* malevolence and Volney Gay (2001) posits that the readiness to receive joy requires an ego that can see and hold together mourning and joy. Even country music recognizes that joy and suffering, pain and dancing go together!

The human dance in between autonomy and belonging, in between myth and parable, in between finitude/limitation and joy, is attended not only by the spontaneous dancers, but by more intentional participants who at least occasionally interpret what is going on. Some of these interpretations follow.

SUSPICIOUS OF JOY

There is no doubt but that an onslaught of negativity envelops many of the contexts of human existence. Nor is there doubt that soured utopian expectations have led to cynicism and bitterness. Some are exhausted by pessimism and the vitalities of hope about futures have been diminished.

This may be a condition endemic within my circle of liberal friends and pastoral caregivers and theologians who live within cultural analyses of economic discrepancies, ecological deteriorations, political disenfranchisements, violence on a global and local scale and within religions who speak of peace and God, unimaginable pluralisms and diversities that seem to lead to moral relativisms, and scientific and technological developments that appear to raise moral issues unprecedented in human history. The continuing presence of racism, sexism, and impediments to the inclusion of sexual and disabled minorities affect this pervasive heaviness. It should not be surprising that living within such perspectives, *and with the sense that one* should *be able to make them better*, is not only disheartening, but a heavy burden. Within that lifestyle, experiences of joy may be viewed as inauthentic, superficial to the depth problems of the human situation, and related to a simplified faithfulness whose primary concern is of individual salvation, viewed as avoiding the complex thickness of the social issues.

Professionals in pastoral care may spend so much time with authentic suffering, with persons whose situations do not get better, with situations in which they experience their own impotence, that a suspicion may develop that such *is* the totality of the human situation, and that alternate experiences must be superficial, trite, inauthentic. Thus some psychiatrists become suicidal, some pastors burn out; some cultural analyses view only the violent or depersonalized dimensions of a culture. A chaplain in a children's hospital experiences hundreds of deaths of children a year. Someone on an obstetrics service attends every stillbirth.

I have heard a rabbi explain his vocation as making "whole the joys and tribulations of life by binding them to a transcendent God." While I would need to discuss with him what he means by "transcendent," I, too, am seeking to define the peculiar callings of pastoral care as witnessing to joy and the goodness of God with tribulations integral and not accidental, with even horrendous evils unable to negate the greater fact of God's goodness.

At times I wonder if this suspiciousness of joy does not uniquely reside in a relatively small and affluent culture that believes that God identifies with the poor and thus those in this culture experience profound shame and guilt at their own wealth. This culture sometimes fears moral centeredness because it disdains moralisms, but affirms pluralisms. That culture somehow expects it should and could change all of this, but experiences hopelessness at its own impotencies. Such a culture may indeed turn toward cynicism and disdain, further diminishing senses of gratitude and joy.

Elie Wiesel (Schuster, Metz, Wiesel, & Boschert-Kimmig, 1999) names hope as the quality that allows for joy…perhaps even within or following a death camp experience. When our students at Eden Theological Seminary return from their first Third World experiences, they almost all comment on the joy that they experienced among the folk with whom they shared life for a very brief time. In my last introductory Doctor of Ministry class, the only international student, from Kenyan poverty, was also the only student to frame his worship offering around joy and the goodness of God. He and another student, from Ghana, in my family dynamics class, stated their bemusement at the heaviness of the dynamics we were exploring and the amount of discontent and turmoil amid family life in a culture that they experienced as affluent. Perhaps a dimension of the liberal's suspiciousness of joy is bred in the bone that refuses finitude and limitation, and carries the expectation of being able to remake a world where joy is guaranteed—rather than living in one where joy is both reality and gift.

SURPRISED BY JOY

Perhaps if a dimension of pastoral care's tasks was to make room for joy, we would all be surprised as to the many places where it would be found. Nouwen would see it in God's great joy at finding the one who was lost rather than wallowing in the many who did not (yet) turn home. The few studies on the dynamics of joy appear to set two requirements for that experience to break through. The first is to be able to hold together differing views of the world, that is—for Volney Gay—mourning and joy. If creatures are destined to live through years of varying stages of grieving, they may not be able to see/experience joy that has been interpreted as somehow coming later. Although still grieving, the mothers who gave birth following the loss of their husbands on September 11 yet experienced great joy. God's joy at the prodigal's return surely sustains God with hope (Wiesel's prerequisite for joy!) even in the midst of the many who do not return.

For Gay, (2001) by defining neurosis as the absence of joy, the neurotic one seeks to be in control and to be self-protective, thus well defended against the possibility of being overcome with feelings of openness and spontaneity, anticipation and entering into the mystery of the unknown. Experiences of ordinary joy are blocked by the neurotic's misperceptions of temporality and connectedness. This person must control time and solve problems. No surprises there! We might note that the fear of the malevolent might defend one solidly from the light touch of the benevolent, two faces of the religious experience, two forces surrounding the creature's everyday experience. My first-year students tend to be sentimental when they speak about the joy they experience in helping others. Somehow, I do not want to take that from them, even as I seek to open them to quite dreadful experiences where they can stand without illusion, and yet with trust, in being open to futures even while fully aware of history and of the present tumultuous experience. Even when therapeutically defined, perhaps pastoral care is at its best when it seeks ways to open the neurotic to being surprised by joy as the creature takes risk in relaxing control and dynamics of self-protection.

Those desperately needing to retain fantasies of dominance and self control, while avoiding terror and disorganization, use up energies that might be devoted to playfulness and to letting things be; that is, trying to be God is not only a losing battle, but one loses one's human gifts of play and joy in the process.

If, then, neurosis and joy are incompatible, it makes great sense that pastoral care ministries may help persons consent to a creaturely stance where they need not keep trying to be God by being in control and having to move from solving one problem to solving another. That ministers themselves almost invariably do this does not mark this as an easy or felicitous task, or the traditional pastoral role as grounded in joy and playfulness in the goodness of God.

It is important to note that we are not speaking here of the culture of joy—the growth therapies—of the sixties and seventies. Those literatures tended to view the creature as oppressed by culture (*Parent*), out of touch with one's own spontaneity and growth potential (*Child*) and needing to connect with this child in order to experience being an adult. These cultures of joy were generally grounded in an understanding of the human creature as unlimited in potential, being ground down by the forces of nature, history, and culture. Theorists like Carl Rogers tended toward equating evil and culture, sin and finitude.

But to be surprised by joy—as Nouwen was among a community of persons who were developmentally disabled—is to consent to not being God and to being able to lean back and forth between the melancholia of finitude and the joy of possibilities.

THE SACRIFICES AND SUFFERINGS OF JOY

Pastoral care might take intellectual leadership in revisiting notions of sacrifice as one of the dimensions of wholeness, rather than as imposition upon a growing ego or a political constraint placed upon one gender by another. At some primal level, God's sacrifice might speak of intentional self-giving on behalf of others, rather than only of a faith grounded in violence, followed by generations of theological interpretations that make sacrifice itself a violent act, and both sacrifice and suffering peculiar to the feminine role.

This suspiciousness of sacrifice is well grounded and legitimate. It has also carried disastrous consequences upon positive processes of negotiating human relationships on behalf of some greater good. Browning's (1997) recent attempts to build in the necessary sacrifice two parents must make to raise children have not met with universal regard among his peers. To sacrifice, somehow, for another, has centuries of misuse against it. Yet placed upon the impossible/possible plane of equality, a knowledgeable pastoral care will perhaps discern that all relationships are based on some form of negotiation, letting be, letting go, yes, giving up for another. At one point there was a tremendous generation gap between the older generation of clergy wives and the younger generation of clergywomen. Many of these older sisters found great joy in their marriages and lay ministries. Similarly, there are women who choose to remain at home in child rearing, sometimes thought of as sacrificing too much of themselves for their children.

For the Christian, the language of sacrifice is historically embedded in the language of joy. A redefinition of the former—in the name of negotiations necessary in history to embody the creature's relationality as well as to recognize its finitude and limitation—may well uncover buried feelings of joy that have been withheld because of embarrassment. I, for example, continue to find joy in the sacrifices I have made for my adult children. Even more so, I find joy in their companionship that would not be possible if I had not let some things go. These sacrifices were small delights or efforts, or speak directly of what could not be in order that something else was possible.

No doubt, complex interfaith and political negotiations carry within them as well some dimensions of sacrifice, caught up as they are in dynamics of control and self-protection, heaviness and the absence of joy. In some worlds, words like *compromise* and *negotiation* have come to mean giving in or letting down. In my world they may mean "making possible."

Sustained by Joy, Especially Its "We" Dimensions

The practices of joy are a dimension of spiritual discipline. Yes, they come as gift, and, yes, they come about through practices of hospitality and little kindnesses, graciousness in the midst of a stress-filled environment, time to notice when there is no time, and remembrance of little moments or glances or recognitions that have made a difference in one's own life. Indeed this is one of the simplest yet deepest offerings of congregational life: being sustained through shared joys; being gathered together, as "we" in the communal nature of sacraments and sacramental moments; finding belonging in shared meaning worlds; and calling and being called by name. These are no simple gifts in a stress-filled and fast-moving society—as they were not in the particular cultural problematics of earlier periods of history. For the hassled farm family doing battle with undeveloped land in the last part of the nineteenth century, through the abandoned teenager on the streets of the city, church—at its best—knows names and offers place, carries hope when all seems lost, receives you when no one else will, and may even share in a moment of joy that both recipient and offerer will carry with them for some time to come.

Pastoral Care as Making Room for Joy

Trying to be God is not only a losing battle, but one also loses one's human gifts of joy and play in the process. Those desperately needing to retain fantasies of domination and self-control, while avoiding terror and disorganization, must use up energies that might be better devoted to playfulness and to letting things be. For, speaking psycho-therapeutically, if neurosis and joy are incompatible, it makes great sense that pastoral care ministries may help persons consent to a creaturely stance in which they need not keep trying to be God by being in control and having to move from solving one problem after another. Some of the dynamics of guilt and shame, which appear to be endemic to the contemporary Christian, may diminish with the unexpected result of there being more energies available for reflection, relationship, and justice making, rather than less.

Speaking theologically, if the creature does not need to be God, the reality of one's own finitude and limitation may be viewed in some of its positive dimensions. Many chronically ill persons experience great joy, as we hear when they begin to be invited to share their stories. At least some of the oppressed leap with joy even prior to the total removal of that which oppresses. The stress many African Americans have experienced in having to live in two worlds has also carried with it some feelings of accomplishment and confidence, delights and devotions. Some of the stories of those experiencing various disabilities carry tales of meaningful relationships, profound spiritual and aesthetic experiences, a celebratory stance toward the accomplishment of what to others appear to be little things. There are very ordinary pastors (from the outside) who continue to have quite extraordinary ministries, although they have never made it through the bureaucracies. The reasons for this are quite simple indeed. Cultural and theological dynamics suggest that the dynamics of readiness to receive joy require a creature that can see and hold together mourning and joy, the reality of one's finitude and limitation with the reality of one's possibilities and pleasures. Creatures can hold different affective states together, and be able to move between them without loss of integrity. Both melancholia and joy must be received; if we become trapped in having to control existence and please others, whether other creatures or God, there is no room left over for joy. There is limited openness to receive experiences other than those of control and self-protection. One loses—or does not develop—the capacity to see the many positive affects and attributes that exist within relationships and cultures. And without experiences of joy, the capacity to receive and trust in the goodness of God—not abstractly, but as it pertains to oneself—can diminish, become debilitated, or, for that matter, never develop at all.

The Goodness of God

Pastoral care and its many practices are grounded in a faith claim affirming the goodness of God. This God is in the world and yet not identified by it, intends the flourishing of the beloved creatures, and affirms their desires for free play in a good world.

Pastoral care affirms that this claim cuts across varying historical and cultural contexts, and that its practitioners throughout the ages have represented that good God in God's mission toward and within that created world. Thus the practices of pastoral care, as variously defined throughout the history of the church, have sought in various ways to embody that good God who not only loves the entirely beautiful creatures, but desires to be loved by them. To claim that contemporary pastoral care practices are to bear witness to joy and the goodness of God is a solidly grounded claim.

At the same time, the reality of the human creature as finite and limited; historically situated; and vulnerable to suffering, violence, and evil cuts through historical time and context. God's entirely beautiful creatures participate in death and dying, loss, grief and mourning, situations of chronicity and violence...horrors of Holocaust and natural disasters, all of the quite human situations that have been taken seriously in the first two movements. The focus of pastoral care on these situations, along with its contemporary participation in attempts to cure, fix, make right, correct the various vulnerabilities, seems to have diminished the discipline's firm grounding in the faith claim as to the goodness of God.

One effect of this has been a failure to use the theological and ritual resources of the faith that point to and make real the goodness of God—that is, dynamic understandings of Incarnation, Trinity, sacrifice, scandal of particularity—and contribute to constructive definitions of them and their relevance to caring practices. Another has been the neglect of the grounding of the practitioners of care in the goodness of God even in the midst of a world such as this, and the failure to develop an integrity of presence and invitation for the beloved creatures to experience joy and goodness even as they consent to their creatureliness and limitation of structure. The flaw (if any) has been placed in the Divine Goodness rather than within the created structure of the creature and the dynamic pulsating temporalities of all that makes up historical existence.

Thus practitioners of pastoral care should have been the primary theologians of theodicy, familiar as we are with the perennial human cry: *Why did God do this to me?* Often this has placed us in the position of being defenders of God and God's assumed powers and actions. God has been on trial, with us as defense attorneys! We try to get God off the hook when God is blamed, either for purported actions or withholding of actions. An entire litany has been presented over the centuries as to how pastoral care practitioners have accounted for God. One will still hear versions of the deeply grounded perspectives: God's ways are mysterious; after awhile, we'll know all about it and understand why. Death came into the world through sin; bad actions, known or unknown, will be punished. We do not yet understand, but in our unfolding reason and research we will know by the next generation. There is no God…for how could any semblance of a loving God allow for…whatever has occurred that does not match the creature's expectations. It is no wonder that pastoral care practitioners have been themselves vulnerable to perspectives, programs, and promises to make things right. We have identified with secular utopias as well as with liberation and political movements that promise lands of milk and honey. Most of us have forgotten how the founders of transactional analysis promised a peaceful world if the leaders at the United Nations could be taught T.A. concepts. Complexes of knowledge seek solutions to the human situation, and our recent history has perceptively become critical of participation in the psychological captivity of pastoral care, the cultural triumph of the therapeutic. More recently—and probably as yet uncritically—we have participated in the various hermeneutics of suspicion that ground what is wrong in economic exploitation, political chicanery, and intentional oppressions by the powerful, which is deeply embedded within the social structures of the culture that is itself viewed as international leader in the contemporary professional disciplines of pastoral care, counseling and theology, and the emerging approaches of practical theology and the practices of ministry!

To claim that pastoral care is about witnessing to joy and the goodness of God is to connect pastoral care's particular and concrete focus on the creatures' lives and situations with the central faith claims of God's mission. It is not to avoid the various analytics of structural oppression. Claims that culture itself is grounded in violence must be considered, particularly within the perspectives of these essays, which begin by defining the creature's situation as fraught with peril.

But three alternate claims ground this perspective on the goodness of God even in the recognition of cultural violence and horrendous evils. The flaw, as noted, is not in the Divine Goodness but in the necessary structure of the creature and the dynamics of both physical and historical creation. There is a necessary givenness in creaturely existence, which, of course, carries with it continuing struggles to find and create the possibilities to be wrought out by limited creatures in the midst of situations that they cannot completely understand. With creatureliness goes, in Meland's felicitous phrase, only "margins of intelligibility." It is fully understandable (at least to me!) that within such a context the creature should seek to define the goodness of God with the creature's own norms for what is viewed as the good of the creature! This is itself, of course, a refusal of creatureliness!

Seeking creaturely consent to the givenness of its creation is not to consent to its "as-isness" or continuation. Carried here are the delicate dances and negotiations so well expressed in the Serenity Prayer, asking to find serenity in the wisdom to perceive what can and cannot be changed. The efficacy of this approach can certainly be claimed by pastoral practitioners who have not yet found an alternative modality. For the person saying this prayer at an AA meeting, the creature is *both* alcoholic and free, consenting to limitation and exerting choice, finding discipline and community. Later I will suggest other models of such consent and continuation in futures that do not insist upon cure in order to experience the goodness of God.

In terms of contemporary practices of care, to consent to real and perceived oppressions and other defined identities is not to surrender to them or give up daily participation in personal and social movements toward justice. It is rather to consent to the givenness of one's present situation that can neither be refused by returning to an earlier period of history or redeemed by the proclamation of a new utopia. Creatures caught in such situations give up too much if they await the goodness of God to be present only in the removal of, say, racism or sexism. Indeed, the presence of joy within liberation movements and deprived communities speaks of the creature's freedom to play and live on despite their various captivities! Surely this is good news.

The co-creation of those structures within which the goodness of God may be more apparent to the creature than the historic reality in which one actually lives is, then, the task rather than the given. The tasks themselves are undertakings of joy and embodiments of God's goodness. It is in this sense that Nouwen insists that the opposite of joy is not realism but rather cynicism. Pastoral practitioners must have courage to absorb the reality of the creature's perils and awfulness...*and* be present to see the vastness of other blessings and emerging possibilities. Acceding to one's creatureliness carries the courage to be within it along with characteristics of persisting, resisting, enduring. Accompanying such a process is delight in the joys of creaturely existence, even celebration, and without guilt or shame that the entire creation is not yet fulfilled (as the creature would expect).

Within a theological perspective that affirms that both ultimacy and immediacy *and* suffering and joy traffic together in the creature's pilgrimage throughout history, we turn to reflections on the goodness of God from within the practices of pastoral care: first, perspectives from caring experiences; second, pastoral care and the religious impulse; third, the dynamics of power and goodness in the definition of Deity; and fourth, the "More" and its relation to joy, goodness, and play.

Some Perspectives from the Practices of Care

That a fellow creature is present when the manifold shocks of experiencing finitude and limitation occur is itself witness to the goodness of God. Through God's goodness the beloved and beautiful creatures are not abandoned, forgotten, despised, or subjected to ontological shame. Pastoral care practices that refuse to abandon the forgotten elderly, the difficult teenagers, the abused women and children, the homeless men and families, or the starving refugees carry the promise of goodness into the daily practices of struggling to care in the perilous world in which we have been placed. Indeed, care is a burden. It is not only a blessing but a necessity that care goes with humanness and not with ordination or certification, for that assures the possibility of a caring presence—there are many of us! Here the creature's perennial question is encountered: *Why has God done this to me?* What kind of a God allows for (fill in the difficulty)? The goodness of God penetrates where creatures live out their daily burdens and experience the grueling challenges of relationship. Perhaps the greatest challenge of contemporary pastoral care is to place caring creatures with hurting creatures in order that the goodness of God can be a more frequently experienced embodied presence.

The caregiver is present in a godly way when the creature learns of how much of meaningful existence is wrought out and not simply given. To find a life is the task; to state or repeat the vision does not penetrate within the complex interconnections of creaturely existence. Pastoral care knows all about the importance of presence over time, through struggles and oppressions, journeys without apparent destination, and periods of unbearable stress. We can affirm God's goodness in the midst of exodus, with the grieving following the hurricane, when the enemy is gathering, and when one feels all alone. Of all of the disciplines, pastoral care knows all too well the reality of resistance to change, perpetuation of violence, refusal of grace and newness, the loss of patience, the truthfulness of "won'ts" and not simply "can'ts." Pastoral care can be realistic and joyful; it does not need to be cynical and depressed.

A retired pastor told me of his presence with an adolescent grandson during a tumultuous divorce of the parents. He later came to understand his role as securing the child—God's goodness present in the embodied and present grandfather, blessed by being retired, God's divine and ultimate goodness embodied in the very particular and concrete situation. The time required was more than therapeutic presence; the patience offered was of sacrificial quality; the ordinariness was of everyday existence wrought out and not given. This man entered into finitude and limitation and found joy and blessing beyond himself.

Pastoral care bears witness not only to the radical vulnerability of the creature, but also to the creature's amazing tenacity and stick-to-itiveness, patience and endurance, and refusals to go away mad. In caring perspectives that focus only upon suffering—or that trivialize or politicize all stories of sacrifice—the stories of those who bear suffering without loss of dignity become forgotten, as do the stories of quiet ones who live out their daily lives without fanfare. For, as with the dynamics of joy, receptivity to the goodness of God must be open to surprises, able to let go control of expected outcomes, and hold a perspective on what, after all, the norms are. Perhaps my norm for God's goodness is that I rise from my wheelchair, an expectation that may keep me from perceiving the many blessings that *do* attend my life. The goodness of God has become connected to having a good life, that is, one without the shocks described in these essays.

Human creatures are developmental organisms, soul and body enfleshed together. And the organism develops within cultural and historical contexts that shape its capacities. Within these parameters of what might be called impaired freedom (for who experiences a freedom unaffected by circumstance or capability?), gracious acts of goodness are offered freely, if humbly. I have sometimes turned my back on these for they seemed beneath my need, and the offerer not on my level. The radical claim of what it means for the giver and receiver to be one may escape us. I may have missed expressions of joy and goodness that were actually present. After my husband's death it was a toss up whether my psychiatrist or the ordinary students who dropped by to watch football games with me contributed the most to my future.

To begin with such witness to God's goodness might appear sentimental and naive, more like a greeting card than a scriptural tale, more akin to refusing horror than to viewing it and, even in its presence, loving God. But there are deeper groundings for such a view. Let us turn to those after reflecting on this poem by Emily Dickinson.

> They might not need me—yet they might—
> I'll let my heart remain in sight—
> A skill so small as mine might be
> Precisely their necessity—

The Creature's Religious Impulse

The practices of pastoral care have been far removed from primary interest in the nature of religious experience. The focus has been on personality theory and developmental thought as the primary tools for interpretation; and, more recently, on other social sciences and liberation perspectives. Few practicing pastors have had courses on the nature of religious experience, although growing focus upon story and narrative has led to story telling about the religious pilgrimage. There is growing recognition that different sensibilities about religious experience may affect persons' preferences for liturgical styles. A recent interest in spirituality has rekindled some connections with experiences of the Holy, but this appears to be more related to personal enrichment than to reflection upon the experiences themselves and what they might suggest about the ways in which the creature experiences the reality of God.

Nevertheless, few seminaries or clinical training programs offer work in the area of religious experience, its history, and its formative influences. Even the creative suggestions of leaders in our own discipline have been neglected. While thanks to Gerkin we continue to reflect on his concept of "living human documents," Anton Boisen's rich explorations of the relationships between mental illness and religious experience have been forgotten (see, for example, *Out of the Depths, Explorations of the Inner World*). Similarly, while Pruyser's work on "The Minister as Diagnostician" has been carried on in the contemporary work of Ramsay, his excellent studies of the nature of religious experience have generally remained on our shelves along with William James and theorists in the history of religion and the psychology of religion.

The vulnerability that lies at the core of human experience is what is disclosed through pondering the creature's religious impulse. The experience of creatureliness is at the center, an awareness of one's place in an unfathomable universe, with feelings that have been conceptualized as awe, terror, trembling before the Holy; with sensibilities that there is something beyond which is wholly, totally, or radically Other. For contemporary pastoral care theorists, theologians who ground their work in the creature's experiences of anxiety that lead to efforts to secure one's place—perhaps to act like God—have been formative. In psychoanalytic terms, one seeks to control time and connections, which can limit the capacity to receive joy and celebrate goodness…including the goodness of God.

Pruyser finds the creature caught up in alternative experiences of benevolence and malevolence. Because of the biological structure of the organism, full comprehension of the creature's place cannot be achieved. Pruyser insists that the creature seeks not after abstract principles but rather, most hopefully, seeks a Presence that intends something good directed toward *me*. Thus the religious impulse has to do with my own lot, not the abstractions of philosophers and theologians. I desire—need—to know the Other's intentions toward me.

The power of this impulse in the forming of the creature's identity makes it difficult for the creature to fathom a world without one's own self. It is so deep as to begrudge knowledge of the many worlds where what happens to me does not matter. When my husband died suddenly, only my world was devastated. Life went on. In Auden's poem about Icarus, nobody notices the boy falling out of the sky. This primary and primal experience—in manifold forms—is what lies behind the creature's stories and interpretations of the world. It grounds the capacities to receive and be eager to interpret the shocks of finitude. The same powerful feelings energize overpowering experiences or intimations of love and belonging, awe and wonder, goodness and a sense that it's all right…even that this is the best of all powerful worlds.

Pastoral care can become better informed about this style of experiencing the world and some Other's intent toward oneself. Herein lay some commonalities in being able to address experiences of the goodness of God. We see that there are many ways to draw upon the goodness of this God, and many faith stories to learn and to tell. The divine stories fashioned out of that religious impulse can be connected to contemporary human stories as, indeed, has been the case throughout history. This provides some connection to creatures who have not been raised in the church but whose lives have nevertheless been touched by this type of experiencing, frequently an active presence within the culture. Meland argues that the faith is carried not only in the individual and the cultus, that is, the church, but also deep within the textures of the culture where the impulses have been connected in relationships and social structures throughout human history.

These cultural connections are what the unchurched young people in prisons and residential treatment centers have overheard. In countries—or regional settings—where the church has been a powerful force in the culture, its themes have interpenetrated secular worlds. To further complicate the issue, it is possible that the biochemical composition of some creatures predisposes them to see the glass half empty rather than half full. Some may have to struggle harder through melancholia to make room for joy. It may be difficult for some—even professionals—to comprehend the depths of depression that may attend some experiences on this level.

And it may well be that some theological shapings of the fruits of these religious impulses prevent participants from celebrations of joy and goodness. For example, if theology has made of death and dying experiences of punishment and sin, the capacity to be surprised by joy in the midst of finitude is diluted. Where theology has made false promises and offered a life of entitlement to good for those who are faithful, the souring of these utopian expectations—as life is actually experienced—can turn one toward cynicism and bitterness. Yet the religious impulse will vary tremendously among those who have lived in the midst of wars or liberation struggles.

On Getting Power and Goodness Together... in a World Such as This

That the creature is continually subjected to the various shocks of finitude makes the theological issue of theodicy a central theme for pastoral care. Which is to be defined: God's power or God's goodness? How are they to be reconciled?

The religious sensibilities hunger for an all-powerful God to secure "me and my household—in ways that I define." This same sensibility can lead to the exclusion of other creatures (sometimes including those within one's own biological family). This primary refusal of creatureliness is integral with being born into givenness—the givenness of a particular body, family, culture, historical time period—along with the capacity to imagine other forms. In normal developmental process, we want parents we don't have, often a God we don't have, and, as we age, frequently a government we don't have! Pastoral care occurs within this dilemma.

Thus a church has to become vulnerable to work out how to live faithfully within their historic time and the limitations of their folk. In my Nashville church, for example, desiring to be a caring—that is, good—community representing a God of equality, grace, and goodness, they had to work out their way of living in the givenness of their historical situation. They found that they could neither simply announce God's point of view, nor experience God's goodness (faithfulness) without tears and suffering. Whether by design or evolution, any flaw did not lie in the Divine Will but in the limited structure of the creature living in the givenness of creation.

The traditional questions: "How does a good God let (fill in the difficulty) happen?" and "What is the meaning of God's power if it is not used in this situation?" were reformulated. Worship continued to celebrate gratitude at being here at all! Energies were refocused from a religious impulse to transcend their historical situation, to a desire to learn how to live within it, as creatures. The conversations did not focus around protecting or defending God, but rather on understanding the complexities of creation itself, and the congregation's limited but crucial role within it.

They were guided throughout by a very deep perception into the role of Jesus Christ as experiencing the human plight from within, from inside, by joining it. In a perilous situation, Jesus received inordinate powers that threatened to overwhelm him, suffered without cynicism, entered into givenness, and found joy and meaning and the goodness of God that was worth passing on to future generations. This brilliant Christian perception got finitude, suffering, and joy together, as they must be newly and continually connected in ordinary family life and the living out of the witness of a faithful church. The crucifixion did not fix the world—except at the highest level of abstraction. Rather, it invited folk to live within it with new depths of understanding of their own situations. "Gentle might" replaced triumphal conquering as a way to live in ordinary time. Throughout history common folk and the churches themselves have realized that there is a cost to changing structures and interpretations, which is a dimension of what is intended in speaking of understanding creation rather than either transcending it or protecting God from being the causative agent of its many perils.

When the religious sensibility focuses on a powerful God who will make all things right—or, on the other hand, on a good God who offers an entitlement of escape from terror, violence, and suffering if honored—the creature's capacities to live with joy within the given are truncated. And since the complexity of a world such as this exceeds the creature's conceptual capacity, churches themselves often become complicit in urging their followers to always transcend history rather than to practice living with joy and justice within it.

Recent theologies have focused on God's suffering with us. This has been very helpful pastorally for many persons who find themselves not abandoned, but, indeed, connected to a God who truly understands their plight. But this can pose a size problem with the creature's understanding of God. Is there "more" God than the suffering One? Conversations also need to consider that there is more to God than mutual suffering, as important as that is, especially in the field of pastoral care. God also promises more from within the magnificence of creation, which is not defined primarily by *my* personal turmoil. Perhaps God suffers with us in the way that a parent suffers with an adolescent, certainly feeling and remembering the pain and anguish, but continuing to be parent, with more gifts and more promises—and more love—to come.

The issues of theodicy are central in pastoral care, and the entire movement of these essays is intended to cast light upon them and, however modestly, to transform some of their understandings. For the creature, there is gratitude that we are here at all, and that God is with us. There is a readiness for a smiling face to break through from behind what might be perceived as a frowning providence. Nor does it deprive God of power to note that some occurrences in the creature's historical existence simply *are*; they are not acts of punishment, or abandonment, nor is the creature participating in a creation where culture is itself violent and historical existence flawed at its core. Pastoral care has many possibilities for theological conversations with creatures who are, quite simply, trying to figure out who they are and what they can count on.

The Goodness of God—and Allowing for the "More"

As we begin, mark three cautions: First, God, and God's goodness, is not simply that which has not yet been explained; second, the "More" is not to hold out for the omnipotent, omnipresent, etc., God of classical theology, snuck back in through changing terminology; and third, the "More" is not to accommodate God's goodness, somewhere on the farther side of the shocks of finitude—that is, lessening their horribleness.

The expression serves several crucial perspectives for the pastoral caregiver. Surely it grounds the human's creatureliness. The complexity of creation and historic existence simply exceeds the creature's conceptual capacity. This is not bad, a punishment, a flaw that will find correction, or some power play to allow God to keep being God, for within this space we "live more deeply than we know," as Bernard Meland phrased it. The creature lives beyond its own comprehension, and is variously puzzled or perplexed or intrigued and imaginative about that situation. Without giving up its giftedness, the creature finds its margins of intelligibility (limits to rationality or intuition) good enough. That is, gratitude for life itself and its many arenas of possibility—at least more than momentarily—sustains and energizes.

It is in this sense that travail is not allowed to define possibility—either of God or of the creature and the historic situation. The creature's placement in the structures of time allow for its passage and the unfolding of new futures. Nor is any one present moment allowed to represent the whole. Neither my delight when my son was born nor my devastation when my husband died could unilaterally interpret the meaning of my existence. This appreciative awareness of existence itself is seldom nurtured by pastoral caregivers, so often seeking to fix or explain or defend God. A spirit of gratitude ponders the goodness of one's creation in relation to self, other creatures, and God, even through the shocks of finitude and failures of utopian expectations. Appreciation for the "More" frees the creature to live within one's genes, families, cultures, and historical periods without either surrendering to the dimensions of givenness or being seduced or lured into a denial of its limitations or refusals to participate in arenas that may bring forth the "More," or at least more justice, kindness, joy.

This sense of "More" can ground the hope that is a prerequisite for joy. Without explaining or denying "isness," the creature can maintain a radical view of the possibilities of the created universe and its own limits of understanding and changing it. Within this point of view, God does not need defense, as is required by the God who is defined and limited by negative experiences of the creature. Moreover, the creature is freed to lift up the manifold goodnesses that are experienced and need not be embarrassed or feel naïve to press one's positive claims about creation, God, other creatures, and oneself.

All too often the models or norms lifted up for the creature's perceptions of one's own situation fairly reek with utopian expectations, images of realized eschatology, and entitlements as to the way creatures should turn out. The failure to offer alternative models from within the various practices of pastoral care reflects our own lack of confidence in that which we actually do. Looking to disciplines that promise the "moreness of utopia," we neglect to present the ways in which creatures can both receive their particular shocks of finitude *and* experience and hold out for joy and the goodness of God.

In quite ordinary time, sufferers of various limitations both receive finitude and celebrate possibility. For example, a student at Eden Seminary presents her rigid and fragile body as only one dimension of who she is—reflecting on how few see her as an attorney and faithful Christian, as one desiring to serve others even as her situation requires a full-time attendant. The millions of persons with chronic illnesses are better models for the human situation than the anticipations of who we should be becoming at the "higher" ends of various developmental and moral sequential understandings of the human pilgrimage...and its ideal goals.

Our churches are filled with creative aging persons, frequently keeping alive the visions of dying churches in their own communities. The creativities and, yes, even joys of aging processes have been subsumed under the burden of having to account for finitude and limitation. The turn from limitation is so deep among us that most denominations look at churches filled with faithful older persons with scorn, impotence, and a desire to fill them up with those who less clearly represent the finitude of the human situation.

In the many visits that pastoral caregivers make to hospitals and other institutions, they meet underpaid yet faithful lower echelon staff persons who actually perform the care that is received by the residents. The ordinary kindnesses and graciousness of underpaid, undervalued persons, whose own finite situations might overwhelm the pastoral visitors, are never conceptualized as ways in which grace is real and the goodness of God finds presence even when theologians and ordained pastors may appear to have deserted or abandoned the sufferers.

In the present world, the children of professional caregivers are routinely cared for by ordinary and everyday caregivers in daycare centers where the staff is poorly paid and undervalued. Living in a culture where the more hands-on care you offer the less you are valued, pastoral caregivers can at least recognize the "moreness" offered by persons of other races, social classes, and educational levels, which allows us to be about our own fights *against* finitude and limitation.

Moving as we do within liberation movements, millions of African Americans, Hispanics, Latinos, women, and persons of homosexual orientation have paid high prices as they have resisted injustice and persisted toward inclusive community. Yet most remain without bitterness or cynicism, usually unrecognized by more prominent leaders, and embodying virtues of persistence and resistance that have not gotten in the way of their celebrations for their creation and the promises and unfoldings of the goodness of God. In fact, there may be more passionate testimony in minority churches than by those more privileged with power and affluence.

Generally theorists of pastoral care have joined the cultural deniers of finitude and limitation and hence failed to lift up learnings from our own experiences. Thus, unaware, we seem to sometimes view culture itself as grounded in violence and exclusion, and human existence and human history as either the fruits of sin or as themselves primarily embodiments of sin. To affirm otherwise—that is, to affirm joy and the goodness of God—is not sentimental and naïve, but an alternate reading of the human situation that connects theological reflections with the actual practices of pastoral care.

The religious impulse is not only to transcend or transform the human situation, but also to learn how to live with grace and dignity within it. The focus is as much on understanding creation as on protecting God. To live as if there were indeed "yet more truth and light to break forth from the Holy" is neither to refuse the reality of finitude and limitation nor to surrender to givenness without claiming the very real gifts and blessings that accompany creation—viewed whole.

Play, Peace, and Persistence

In these essays I am striving to place suffering, joy, God's goodness, and persistence in the same conversation. Indeed, human reality is awful—perilous, horrible, uncontrollable. Even as I am reviewing this essay, two nightclub tragedies, a gasoline storage barge explosion, and countless other shocks of finitude and limitation are preoccupying the creature's reflections. Some we miss entirely—as devastating earthquakes in China occur beyond our ken. Pastoral care's reflections have focused on such sufferings, including those of natural causation, from genes and developmental or aging processes, from unintended consequences of long ago decisions (often, not even one's own) and changes in one party of a relationship (or one group within a community) without changes in the other.

To introduce play into these dilemmas may appear naïve and even cruel. Yet the essays insist upon the "moreness" of creation and the goodness of God even here, and especially expressed in the various acts of compassion and care that accompany and attend the horrors.

Joy, goodness, and play do not occur in some separate realm, or happen upon the whim of an absent, omnipotent god. Their reality is *in* the human situation of finitude and limitation, caughtness within genes, chronicity, disaster, and horror, for the mystery of God is affirmed as deeper than that of evil and circumstance. When suffering, joy and goodness, and play and persistence are placed together, God is experienced at the margins of the inevitability of ongoingness. Over time, contingency becomes a gift rather than a curse.

Yet the above paragraph is not only a faith statement, to be denied or held to accountability as any faith statement. Certainly it is rooted in the goodness of God as the prior fact, and creatureliness (including mortality) the primary definition of human being. Certainly it expects the creature to sense, intuit, and experience some appreciative awareness of the gift of life itself, along with the immensities of creation and culture that both surround and define oneself.

But it is more than a faith statement: It is a recognition that no one experiences the whole of reality, and that pastoral care's data of suffering and anxiety, pervasive depression and inequality, occurs within a creation and culture in which there are multitudinous data of joy. Experiences of resilience and grace, or endurance that did not turn to cynicism or despair, and persistence that did not go away mad when its goals were not achieved also mark the creatures' pilgrimages. In many ways, it is the task of pastoral care always to invite the creature to see more of reality than has been acknowledged or has appeared within one's own orbit of meaning. Moreover, even within the various shocks, the creature is hopefully offered comfort, the presence of a fellow sufferer (creature or God), the reality of not being abandoned, and at least signs or reminders of the good, beautiful, whole possibility that attend and accompany the perils. It is in these intermediate spaces, these places of "inbetweenness," that play is an appropriate accompaniment to creatureliness.

We will explore this in relation to what we can learn from the play of children; the nature of play as resistance; the fit between play as transitional and the recognition that peace is never a permanent or static condition; and the concept that a dimension of pastoral care's vitality is to offer understandings that suffering, joy, goodness, and persistence traffic together—and are wrought out in the creature's lifetime searches for what it means to be creature, not God.

The Play of Children

I watch the children who attend my daughter's day-care center play—and realize that I am observing them learning. I learn from my daughter that infants and toddlers are neither naïve innocents nor passion-driven beings to be tamed. I realize that from birth they are learning how to connect to an environment that is alien, and, as I observe, I recognize how many of their connections come through play. I observe the play between mother or father and child as they deliver and pick up their child, the playfulness of greeting rituals and tasks, the rituals of touch and rememberings, the recollections of the day—even with the bright-eyed six month old child. I view the playfulness of potty training, and the practices that are taught concerning sharing; the difference between bringing a toy to the day-care center (where you share) and leaving it at home where it is all yours (oh, the risks of human community).

It had been some time since I had recalled Erik Erikson's view of play and its crucial influence on development. With risk and pleasure, children are carving their way through an alien landscape, filled with the need for great persistence in practice and trust that one can make it. The recognition of human difference begins early—genetic structure and family structure, expectations of social class and learning about relationships—all of this is going on before my eyes! For the first time the day care enrolls a child with a Mommy and a Mama, and the child learns about Daddies while the others play naturally with the children of same-sex couples. And one child is already learning a second language because of her mother's multicultural experiences.

A theologian friend tells me of the different ways in which his two children enter into the pastoral care work that they do through their church. In taking meals to elderly persons who are in need emotionally as well as physically, one child gallops in, greets the older person with a combination of delight and intrigue, and makes himself at home. The other child enters cautiously, participates reluctantly, appears to be analyzing the situation and making her choices as to what to do. Once, when they left after a visit, she had a list of ideas as to how to fix the room! We laughed about the difference between play and analysis, between a sense of intrigue in entering a new situation and a more cautionary or wary approach. We agreed that both were necessary.

How has pastoral care missed so much of this playful style? Certainly those who read Winnicott (1989) and can converse about transitional objects are aware of it, but there is more at stake than that therapeutic usage. Perhaps we have not learned much about the playfulness of learning about care from children because we have, until recently, done only limited work with children. Educators have worked with children more than we have; even the best of church related day-care centers have had limited pastoral care practitioners; many of children's problems have been referred to specialists, including children subjected to abuse for whom the profession of preference became social work!

There may be a connection here between an earlier interpretation: that those who provide the most hands-on care in our culture receive the lowest wages. A caring focus upon professionals and trained persons could easily miss the importance of play in learning and care with children. One of the most interesting workshops I attended recently was by a person who worked solely with dying children, guiding their play in connection with their hospitalizations and their journeys toward death. The capacity to put play and dying children together is the creative act of creatures connecting to finitude without cynicism.

A similar absence has marked our learnings about play and pleasure among persons who are severely disabled. Focusing on suffering and unfairness, we may have missed that limitation and even a severe condition of disability need not determine the quality of life, including its pleasures and desire, playfulness and appreciation of goodness and beauty, possibility and welcome boundaries. My student who is the most severely disabled—her disabilities forcing her out of a degree program which she loves—speaks with passion about experiencing the goodness of God in her life, and writes newsletters (with great difficulty) that are filled with humor and insight. She plays in the interim space between her physical reality and her imagination, creating worlds that are both real and allow for playfulness. In such ways she participates in her existence, co-creating its frame.

Perhaps theologians have made too heavy the imprecation to "put away childish things," and dismissed playfulness from the various gravities and shocks of the human situation. But this truncates the rich area of "inbetween"—where imagination and reality meet and some sense is made of them: perhaps a new game, perhaps a ritual, perhaps a gesture worth repeating. For the child, a creative act occurs within the very space where there is a lack of knowing—for the person with severe disabilities, the imperfection and its very awkwardnesses call forth alternate ways of seeing and managing.

How can such playfulness—so central in human development— not be an integral dimension of the creature learning how to live within the new situations that new concepts have established for us: globalization, pluralism and diversity, scientific discoveries, even violence? Perhaps in some ways we are like the infant seeking to carve our way through an alien landscape. Perhaps we can't count on the kinds of formal learnings of technical rationality that deceptively promise human betterment in the form of control over the passages of time and culture.

Play as Resistance

For children, play is central to their participation in the sheer act of living. The neurotic's anxiety about security may hamper the sense of play—as it gets in the way of joy. Those in charge may prematurely control the play, whether its experimentations, boundary pushing, or its exuberance. For the adolescent, some forms of play may demonstrate resistance against what is perceived as parental control. For the oppressed, play may be a crucial way of claiming their own realities and, hence, be dangerous to the oppressor. The history of slavery discloses play as resistance, as the slaves gathered in their own communities for singing and dancing, worship and eating. This was no denial of the horribleness of their situation, but rather a claiming of who they could be within it. It is not accidental that in dictatorships the play of the oppressed is carefully controlled—no free play is allowed in Tiananmen Square, and in some countries women are not allowed out alone. At one point in the Roman Catholic Church, sisters had to go out in twos for both self-protection and account-ablility; a playful God or Jesus has not yet been constructed (or deconstructed!) from the priority of God's privileging the poor.

When play became identified with children, its remarkable gifts in lightening anxieties, providing relationships, and inviting participation in one's own world became invisible. It is not unusual to make fun of playfulness in nursing homes, where bingo and singing, art and accomplishments keep the creature in contact with its diminishing worlds. The marriages of old persons are lifted up for humor. Play is difficult for those in control, for at its best it carries no pat answers, for the learnings are in the processes of playfulness itself.

Play can affect the imaginations of both the afflicted and the caregiver, the former as they reach out for participation and the latter as they learn how to see beneath surfaces. We can see the disabled body and not the lawyer who fights for civil rights, or the creative writer who writes plays about the historical Jesus, or the soul and history of thick experiences that have shaped the life of the old man in the wheelchair. "You look at me," he said, "and you see only an ugly old man, but within I am filled with great beauty." This capacity to see resists the stereotyping that can lead to oppression, exclusion, or abandonment.

In this sense, imagination itself has been truncated, for it is not only the vision of how a situation should or could be…but also seeing what is through changed eyes. Resistance is to hope and to play at the edges of consent, not surrender, and hence to resist both the neurosis of seeking control or the surrender of living under an oppressor's rule. A woman writes in *The New York Times* (Herbert 2002) about how her travels into newness following her husband's death gradually eased her pain. Almost forced into playfulness (the alternative being burying herself at home) she resisted a lifetime of mourning, incorporating instead a playful style of moving from mourning to joy and back again…and again…The Special Olympics are another example of play that shapes new worlds for its participants, both athletes and their sponsors.

Play, Persistence, and Peace

In terms of children's play, Western culture has generally opted for order at the price of playfulness. The shift is not unlike the one that has occurred between the free play of children gathering together on vacant lots and forming their own softball games, and the completely organized, adult-driven, controlled scheduling of Little Leagues. The whole notion of play as creating meaning (rules, roles, gods) in strange (transitional) space has been transmuted into the sharing of technical knowledge. Following tragedy, grief teams appear; churches and business leaders are trained in conflict management; booklets inform pastors how to do premarital counseling; and one can observe in shopping malls and during arrivals and departures at day-care centers the influence of differing children's experts on the ways parents and children treat one another.

The result of this shift has been to make the game over too soon. As one learns the rules, historical existence and its management make sense. The expectation is that all will learn and play by the rules that some have established. Play turns into goal setting and outcomes assessment. A church will achieve the "right" inclusive community. Proper premarital counseling will lead to fewer divorces—as indeed, it might. The United Nations will learn a form of discourse that will permanently prevent wars.

Yet remember the dynamics of children's play in unfamiliar space…It occurs in a matrix where everything is changing: their own bodies, the needs of their caregivers, the particular world in which they have been born, whether or not they are the only child playing in the family. Some children tragically learn to play along the way to their dyings, or through the divorces of their beloved parents. The context, at least in the Western world, gradually shifts from play in a nonordered world to opting for order at the price of playfulness: We must ingest knowledge about our worlds and act out of it. The shift is from playfully working it out to grueling attempts to get it right. Much has been lost in the cultural move from play to the world of technical rationality, not the least of which is the loss of an unfortunately sentimentalized, but accurate perspective: it doesn't matter if you win or lose, but how you play the game. The creature in a world of peril and pleasure, stockiness and possibility, requires a sense of play to find integral ways of keeping connected the shocks of finitude and limitation and the joys and goodness of the created world where one is beloved creature and entirely beautiful, even—or especially—as players in givenness.

With this perspective, play is the work of a lifetime. Not only are all good works partial, but the definitions of what they are keep shifting around us! In pastoral care, one does have to experience what appears to be the same situation again and again…never forgetting the freshness of the experience for the one experiencing loss, rejection, being invisible. The misplaced use of the tools of technical reason can miss the thickness and poignancy of a situation…not entering in playfully, but applying rationally.

For the caregiver, this adaptability need not mean the loss of integrity, for it is the integrity that frees one to risk and play! The caregiver will learn that play in one world may not work in another, thus Nouwen found joy in the L'Arche community but not at Harvard or Yale. In pastoral care one will find oneself needing a style of play with those who have been or are being caught on the wrong side of history, those who cannot vote for their church to be open and affirming, those left behind by changing definitions of what is politically correct. Like the children in the vacant lot in the 1930s, there may be no coach to call the team to order, no staff person to announce designated roles.

For such situations, qualities of persistence and resilience can keep the game open-ended and all who show up involved. Pastoral care is filled with situations that could call forth the spirit of play: situations where the pastor/caregiver doesn't know what to do; situations where the pastor/caregiver moves from the world of the deathbed to the world of the birthing room, with little space in between for preparation…This is the transitional space for a playful tone.

Of course, the creature's situation is perilous. Even more so should reflection on it be fresh, creative, and imaginative. Some would argue that it is out of such reflection—and its expression in story, art, even belief—that culture and faith are born. It is not sentimental to lift up the elevator man as caregiver, as Gerkin (1997) does. It is a recognition that building culture comes out of playful experiences and not pronouncement. It is also a recognition that if grace and consent do not lie at the core of relationship, that which is imposed upon it rapidly becomes empty and/or disconnected.

These dynamics of play and persistence can inform our understanding of peace. Peace is not a static condition. Like war, it is composed of dynamics and passages, power and particularities. No more can pastoral care call forth peace than it can rid the world of war. But in its particularities and playfulness, persistence and endurance, it presents an alternative. The finite and limited creature, even in the midst of its sufferings and perils, is not only coming to understand but to learn to live with grace in the world in which it finds itself.

Play and Pastoral Practices

Pastoral care is neither applied theology nor skillful use of the processes of a technical rationality. It is rather participation in the care of the entirely beautiful creatures finding ways to live in the perils of historical existence. And as they persist and resist, suffer and celebrate, form and reform communities, they experience what it means to be co-creators of religion and culture.

A sense of play in those perilous, transitional, as yet unformed (or overformed) spaces is crucial, for one of the creature's gifts is imagination, and we are gifted to see beyond our capacities to enact and control. At the same time, we are lovingly placed in particular bodies and families, nations and cultures, which the imagination can transform much faster than any historical process or technical reason! Yet here everyday existence is wrought out, sometimes only through grueling encounters, and in these very processes gods are worshiped and cultures created. This is where pastoral practices occur.

These essays seek to get suffering, joy, God's goodness, play, finitude, and limitation in the same conversation. What to me is the primary Christian intuition does this; celebration, suffering, persistence, and joy are all dynamics in the events of a Holy Week understood as witness to the goodness of God. This core intuition—which makes Palm Sunday's celebrations integral to the movements of the week— holds the caregiver in the most horrendous of situations even while remembering—or awaiting—experiences of real joy. Thus pastoral care can witness to the joy and the goodness of God with integrity, steeped as it is in the thickness of each creature's historical situation and biological condition. While it would be nice to think that the voice of pastoral care has been so silent in matters of theological construction because of its humility, it is probably more accurate to note that the complexities of its stance are overwhelming. No wonder it has sought after theories to be applied, whether those of the various church disciplines or of the most prominent of contemporary human sciences! No wonder it has fallen under the sway of the procedures of technical rationality, offering ways through grief and conflict, depression and difficult dialogue. And the search—and even the offerings—have been and are helpful—over the long haul. But what is missed might be the most important of all: playful participation in the creation of religion and culture!

But that is the imaginative view...In a realistic perspective, the primary particularity of pastoral care places this creative process within the ordinary, everyday church...within the given, already formed community...ongoing within the dynamic processes of a culture with its history and interpretations, visions and boundaries. Once we mean that pastoral care goes with baptism and not ordination...that it is an act of the creature and not the professional…that each creature is both giver and receiver of care…and that those who do the most hands-on care are probably the most valuable practitioners—then pastoral care has placed itself at the centers where embodiment and renewal actually happen.

Reflections on Knowledge and Formation

Pastoral knowing—and pastoral knowledge—is like the sea. Elizabeth Bishop's poem expresses it well:

It is like what we imagine knowledge to be:
dark, salt, clear, moving, utterly free,
drawn from the cold hard mouth
of the world, derived from the rocky breasts
forever, flowing and drawn, and since
our knowledge is historical, flowing, and flown.

(Bishop 1983, 65)

Pastoral knowing—or pastoral wisdom—refuses easy conceptualization, residing as it does within the layered existence of the human creature. Multigenetic and multicultural, the creature's characteristics insist on particular form. As historical creatures, both history and human creatures refuse to be what concepts from philosophy, theology, science say that they are! These messy intersections of theoretical and practical knowledge are the locations of pastoral care.

The pastor's lens is necessarily interactional and multidisciplinary. The creature's biology and chemistry, development and context are thick and teeming. Rebecca Chopp (1995) has described the "pulsating temporality" in which we live.

Any pastoral situation (like the sea) is deep and complex, international and historical, flowing and flown. It is at these complex intersections of historical existence (perilous places!) where meaning is wrought out and the grueling challenges of embodying the creature's givenness as a relational creature are experienced.

Within this givenness, the creature is also blessed with imagination and creativity, and can envision a life other than the one in which one finds oneself. For some, givenness becomes a curse to be overcome or transformed. For some it is a givenness to be understood in order that it can be controlled. The givenness of death is transformed into eternal life...*for death shall have no dominion.* The complexities and violence of human and cultural interactions will one day be done away with...*the kingdom* (or realm) *of God will come.* For some linear thinkers, issues of causation are made to appear unilateral, so that *if only* that could happen *the peace that passeth understanding* would be normative instead of but one dimension in the flow of historical existence, one reality among many, one emotional state with no guarantee as to its continuance.

Within this perilous morass of givenness, the creature is not only blessed with imagination but is also structurally limited. One experiences—and can grow into—only a margin of intelligibility in comprehending its own context. This is as certain for the post-modern person as for the cave dweller—for the seminary graduate as for the ordinary layperson. Yet in its thick context each creature lives more deeply than it can know...Aware of only a dimension of its own brain and metabolic activity, the creature can scarcely comprehend the multidimensional richness of its context and the ways in which unanticipated consequences flow from earlier actions and reactions. While for some cultures and individuals this is not an issue, for many it is difficult for the creature to consent to having only a margin of intelligibility, instead of knowledge of and control over the whole. Indeed, some languages insist on wholeness as a human norm.

Within this layered existence, then, we find our way, usually wrought out, seldom simply given, frequently engaging in grueling encounters, oftentimes with even the good folk lost and puzzled. It is no wonder that we seek to secure ourselves, seeking control over time and connectedness, space, place, and situation. When the existentialists speak of the anxiety that causes the human to secure itself and so become sinful, I speak of the realistic perils and predicaments of the creation in which we were lovingly placed. There our purpose is to find the joy and sense of God's goodness that is promised, and to speculate less on the Divine Nature than to engage in intentional yet playful learning to find the best—the most caring and the most just—ways to live within that givenness. What may be most important—especially when we seek to define pastoral care as being witness to joy and the goodness of God—is not to limit our perceptions to only one or two lens.

Pastoral Knowledge: Who Wants It?

Theorists, theologians, and practitioners of pastoral care have not always taken with full seriousness the perspectives on the human situation that have grounded these essays. Let us reflect again with Elizabeth Bishop for a metaphor of the knowledge that we carry:

> I have seen it over and over, the same sea, the same,
> slightly, indifferently swinging above the stones,
> icily free above the stones,
> above the stones and then the world.
> If you should dip your hand in,
> your wrist would ache immediately,
> your bones would begin to ache and your hand would burn
> as if the water were a transmutation of fire
> that feeds on stones and burns with a dark gray flame.
> if you tasted it, it would first taste bitter,
> then briney, then surely burn your tongue.
> (Bishop, 1983, 66)

Pastoral knowing, pastoral knowledge, is not generally welcome knowledge. It may taste bitter; burn your hand and tongue. Everybody dies. Most of us develop illness or diseases that do not get better; indeed, we may become worse. Violence is hidden beneath surfaces and erupts unexpectedly. Crises of natural and cultural orders perennially surround us. Individuals and cultures secure themselves against anxiety and insecurity by building barriers around themselves that lead to situations that create more anxiety and disruption. Safe space diminishes; it has left not only airport and office buildings, but home and church. Public discourse is divisive as often as it is healing, as the many differences do not neatly dissolve into inclusive community. That which we have created to secure us itself changes! In the safest of our havens!

The creatures keep following promises that the perils and predicaments are accidental instead of intrinsic. Contemporary disciplines present practices of technical reason that offer conflict management, grief management, stages of grief and development, and complex systems of establishing goals so that we can map our ways to get there. For some of us, we rightly make use of all the cultural resources within our ken: laser for eyesight; dialysis for kidney; elimination of Tay Sachs from my racial group; organ transplants; anti-depressants; programs, promises, and perspectives on our health, wholeness, and well being. When all does not go well, we may reflect endlessly and argumentatively upon the unfairness of Divine Nature or those who have secured themselves at the expense of others. Political systems, economic systems, limited resources for everyone—each takes its role in being the lens to unscramble the messiness, to order or restructure the chaos, to find places with similar households that can do no other but limit the awfulness—and awe-fullness—of God's creation and the flow of history in which human cultures form and reform over time.

Since much of the knowledge of pastoral care is about the particular rather than the abstract, its creators stand in continuing tension with attempts to get things ordered and understood. While the abstractions of racism and sexism are being continually rearranged, pastoral care works with particular situations where theology is not announced or applied, but embodied and practiced slowly and over time. Because of this stance, the discipline of pastoral care stands poised to make at least modest contributions to what some have defined as the central issues of the day: globalization and pluralism/diversity, advances in science and technology, and violence—including violence within the religious impulse and the religious organization. A local pastor connects a small, elderly rural congregation with farmers in an African country, and grows crops, sending the proceeds to Ghana; the pastor brings in a suburban church to help with seed money for both sets of farmers. One church works on issues of pluralism and diversity, even as another parish struggles with the role of the American flag in the sanctuary, how to discuss the war, how to relate to the many crises with teenagers in their neighborhood or community. Pastoral care brings concreteness and particularity to issues that can turn into the rearrangement of abstractions; and the other disciplines can continually keep pastoral care practices grounded and connected with what is going on not only at their margins, but at the core. The many areas of knowledge of the human situation dialogue and practice in the perils and predicaments where pastoral care has its home.

Since our knowledge is like the sea, it is continually changing. In March 2003, the cover page of *The New York Times Magazine* had in bold print: "HALF OF WHAT DOCTORS KNOW IS WRONG." The tracing of medical history is the story of changing knowledge and practices—from leeches to lasers, if you will—and the history of pastoral care discloses the same shifts: from ordained to lay, from unilateral scriptural authority to an awesome integration of scripture, tradition, reason, and experience. The discipline is at present at a creative point in its claiming of its own knowledge bases. From having traditionally applied knowledge from more highly valued disciplines, such as scripture or a human science such as psychology, pastoral care has become an intentionally dialogic discipline in which some of the partners in the dialogue are the recipients of its practices. Deeply grounded theologically in the affirmation that giver and receiver are one, the pastoral imagination is freed to enact caring practices that best fit the great variety of contemporary creatures.

Knowledge has also come from the clinical dimensions of the discipline, focusing around the self-knowledge required of the caregiver. Such deep knowledge continues to be vital, especially as it is not limited to psychological insights, but to the spiritual and theological resources upon which pastoral caregivers uniquely draw—both lay and ordained. Most recently, pastoral care has claimed some of the insights from those studying congregational practices, moving pastoral care into a primary congregational context and also bringing new value to the ordinary and everyday practices by which congregants care for one another and seek to reach out beyond themselves to their neighborhoods, cultures, even global communities.

In these endeavors, there has developed a new intentionality about method, seeking to take the complexity of the contest with full seriousness as a contribution to truthfulness, rather than as an impediment to its clarity. Here the work of Don Browning has been especially helpful, as the practices of care themselves become central in the processes of teasing out the perspectives and transformative possibilities of a fundamental practical theology as the work of theology itself.

But the deepest contribution may be that which is hardest to hear: I once again use the words of the theologian Bernard Meland (1976, 165).

> Elementalism, I would hold, is simply a capacity to acknowledge humbly and humanly this fact of existential limitations defined and symbolized by the events of birth and death, and to experience creaturely feelings appropriate to such limitation and dependence.

Pastoral care bears witness to this fact of death and limitation, expressed in the many arenas for care that frame these essays. Yet the frame itself bears witness to God's presence within each of these extremities, bearing there the suffering and reminding of the "more" that lies as one awaits with patience and endurance. It is not at all ironic that the discipline that lifts up most radically the tensions and sufferings of creaturely existence should also lift up most buoyantly and boldly the reality of the joy and goodness of God to be found— not *even* there, but especially there, as the creature leans always back and forth between joy and melancholia, belief and unbelief, autonomy and dependence, benevolence and malevolence. Perhaps the old hymn could be restored to be sung with delight and hope: "leaning on the everlasting arms." And certainly those arms include ordinary pastoral caregivers.

Issues of Formation

This being the case, I offer modest reflections for conversations about the formation of such caregivers. First, the formation is for a lifetime, not the cure of a situation or event. The human situation is a predicament that is perennial. The image of perpetual care used by cemetery associations comes to mind: persistence in the perpetual care of human creatures in the continuing perils of existence.

Second, the caregivers are themselves to be committed to such a deep faithfulness that they are able to move back and forth through the experiences symbolized in Holy Week (for the Christian): those of celebration, suffering, daily persistence, and joy. The caregiver is a mature leaner, rich in awaiting, grounded in what may appear to be an alternative faithfulness, but which turns out to be the contemporary embodiment of the classical affirmations of God's trustful presence even though we walk through the valley of the shadow of death.

Third, the caregivers need to claim a responsibility for the culture in which they care...not only on behalf of the creatures who live beyond the church, but on behalf of the culture itself, that its positive resources be developed and not disdained, even as work is perennially underway to provide resources for the manifold and unending requirements of the creature.

Finally, conversation must occur about qualities of caregivers: Qualities of persistence, endurance, and courage are necessary. Resilience and buoyancy are desirable. The capacity to absorb is vital, and the freedom to play a primary obligation. Perhaps Sharon Welch (1985) had it right years ago when she presented her trinity for persons working out their faith in a world resistant to becoming what she desired it to be: persist, resist, and celebrate.

Works Cited

Alcor Life Extension Foundation. (2003). Retrieved 29 February, 2003, http://www.alcor.org/

Adams, M. M. (1999). *Horrendous evils and the goodness of God*. Ithaca, N.Y.: Cornell University Press.

Adorno, T. W. (1997). *Dialectic of enlightenment*. London: Blackwell Verso.

Anderson, H., & Foley, E. (1997). *Mighty stories, dangerous rituals: weaving together the human and the divine*. San Francisco: Jossey-Bass.

Auden, W. H., & Mendelson, E. (1991). *Collected poems* (1st Vintage International ed.). New York: Vintage International, Vintage Books.

Bishop, E. (1983). At the fishhouses. In *The complete poems 1927–1979*. New York: Farrar, Straus & Giroux.

Browning, D. S. (1980). *Pluralism and personality: William James and some contemporary cultures of psychology*. Lewisburg, Pa.; London: Bucknell University Press.

—— (1983). *Practical theology*. San Francisco: Harper & Row.

—— (1997). *From culture wars to common ground: religion and the American family debate*. Louisville: Westminster John Knox Press.

Chopp, R. S. (1995). *Saving work: feminist practices of theological education*. Louisville: Westminster John Knox Press.

Clebsch, W. A., & Jaekle, C. R. (1983). *Pastoral care in historical perspective*. New York: J. Aronson; distributed by Scribner Book Companies.

Crossan, J. D. (1975). *The dark interval: towards a theology of story*. Niles, Ill.: Argus Communications.

Dickinson, E. (1976). They might not need me—yet they might. In *Complete poems of Emily Dickinson*. New York: Back Bay Books.

Dudley, C. D. (2002). Congregations serve as beacons of hope. *Christian Century* 119 (14): 20.

Fox, M. (2002). Chiam Potok, 73, Dies; novelist illumined the world of Hasidic journalism. *The New York Times,* 24 July 2002, 17.

Friedman, E. H. (1985). *Generation to generation: family process in church and synagogue.* New York: Guilford Press.

Gay, V. P. (2001). *Joy and the objects of psychoanalysis: literature, belief, and neurosis.* Albany: State University of New York Press.

Gerkin, C. V. (1979). *Crisis experience in modern life: theory and theology in pastoral care.* Nashville: Abingdon Press.

—— (1984). *The living human document: re-visioning pastoral counseling in a hermeneutical mode.* Nashville: Abingdon Press.

—— (1986). *Widening the horizons: pastoral responses to a fragmented society.* Philadelphia: Westminster Press.

—— (1991). *Prophetic pastoral practice: a Christian vision of life together.* Nashville: Abingdon Press.

—— (1997). *An introduction to pastoral care.* Nashville: Abingdon Press.

Gill-Austern, B. L., & Miller-McLemore, B. J. (1999). *Feminist and womanist pastoral theology.* Nashville: Abingdon Press.

Grennan, E. (2002). *Still life with waterfall.* St. Paul: Graywolf Press.

Groome, T. (1991). *Sharing faith: a comprehensive approach to religious education and pastoral ministry: the way of shared praxis.* San Francisco: HarperSanFrancisco.

Herbert, B. (2002). The invisible women. *The New York Times,* 12 September 2002, 27.

Hiltner, S. (1958). *Preface to pastoral theology.* New York: Abingdon Press.

Hodgson, P. (1972). Freedom, dignity, and transcendence: a response to B.F. Skinner. *Soundings* 55 (Fall 1972): 347–58.

James, W. (2004). *The varieties of religious experience: a study in human nature.* New York: Simon & Schuster.

Lane, B. C. (1991). Dragons of the ordinary: the discomfort of common grace. *Christian Century* 108:774.

Marty, M. (2002). Quotidian acts. *Christian Century* 119 (July 3, 2002): 47.

Meland, B. E. (1953). *Faith and culture.* New York: Oxford University Press.

—— (1962). *The realities of faith*. New York: Oxford University Press.

—— (1976). *Fallible forms and symbols*. Philadelphia: Fortress Press.

Moss, H. (1995). Cardinal. *The New Yorker,* 6 November 1995, 88.

Nouwen, H. J. M. (1997). *Adam, God's beloved*. Maryknoll, N.Y.: Orbis Books.

Nuland, S. B. (1994). *How we die: reflections on life's final chapter*. New York: A.A. Knopf ; distributed by Random House, Inc.

Pruyser, P. W. (1976). *The minister as diagnostician: personal problems in pastoral perspective*. Philadelphia: Westminster Press.

Quindlen, A. (2002). One day, now broken in two. *Newsweek* (Sept. 11, 2002): 72.

Ramsay, N. J. (1998). *Pastoral diagnosis: a resource for ministries of care and counseling*. Minneapolis: Fortress Press.

Sandomir, R. (2003). Report says facility beheaded Williams. *The New York Times,* 13 August 2002, 3.

Schuster, E., Metz, J. B., Wiesel, E., & Boschert-Kimmig, R. (1999). *Hope against hope: Johann Baptist Metz and Elie Wiesel speak out on the Holocaust*. New York: Paulist Press.

Slouka, M. (2002). A year later: notes on America's intimations of morality. *Harper's Magazine* (September 2002): 35–43.

Suchocki, M. (1988). *The end of evil: process eschatology in historical context*. Albany: State University of New York Press.

Varshney, A. (1995). *Democracy, development, and the countryside: urban-rural struggles in India*. Cambridge, Eng.; New York: Cambridge University Press.

—— (2002). *Ethnic conflict and civic life: Hindus and Muslims in India*. New Haven, Conn.: Yale University Press.

Volf, M. (1996). *Exclusion and embrace: a theological exploration of identity, otherness, and reconciliation*. Nashville: Abingdon Press.

Welch, S. D. (1985). *Communities of resistance and solidarity: a feminist theology of liberation*. Maryknoll, N.Y.: Orbis Books.

Winnicott, D. W., Winnicott, C., Shepherd, R., & Davis, M. (1989). *Psycho-analytic explorations*. Cambridge, Mass.: Harvard University Press.

Wren, B. (1995). I come with joy. In *Chalice hymnal*. St. Louis: Chalice Press.